REFLECTIONS
of the
HEART

REFLECTIONS
of the
HEART

A Collection of Essays on Life,
Self-Discovery, and Living Joyfully

Ron Roesler

BYBLIO
PRESS
Inspire, Inform,
and Transform

Byblio Press
11410 NE 124th Street
Kirkland, WA 98034 USA
info@bybliopress.com
www.bybliopress.com

Ordering Information: This book may be ordered by contacting the publisher at the address or email above. Special discounts are available on quantity purchases by corporations, associations, and others. For details, contact the publisher at any of the above addresses.

The views expressed in this work are solely those of the author and do not necessarily reflect the views of the publisher, and the publisher hereby disclaims any responsibility for them.

Printed in the United States of America
ISBN: 978-1-964060-30-9 (hc)
ISBN: 978-1-964060-31-6 (sc)
ISBN: 978-1-964060-25-5 (eb)

Library of Congress Control Number: 2025905440

Welcome to my journey of self-discovery.

This book is a collection of essays that
reflect my understanding of the best traits
and behaviors of life and living well!

My personal mission is to make a positive difference
by writing and sharing my perspectives on life,
while living authentically and being true to myself.

CONTENTS

Dedicated to Helène,

My Friend, My Love, My Wife, My Life!

FOREWORD

I have had the privilege of knowing Ron Roesler for over twenty-five years. In that time, I have come to appreciate and admire his character, depth of heart, and unwavering commitment to kindness, humility, and love. Ron entered my life as my stepfather; while formal titles may change, he remains both a father figure and a friend. Our relationship, like any that spans years, has seen its share of laughter, tears, and even moments of healthy debate. Yet, through every high and low, our steadfast bond and deep mutual respect have endured, growing only stronger with time.

Throughout the years, Ron has been a model of integrity, demonstrating an innate kindness and care that extends to everyone in his life. He treated my mother, who has since passed, with remarkable love and respect — a reflection of his gentle, compassionate engagement with the world. Ron lives with a steady, open heart, grounded in positive values that he practices daily, not merely as ideals. His ability to see the best in others, myself included, consistently reminds me of the power of empathy and grace.

While I feel deeply honored to share my perspective on Ron, I recognize that capturing his true essence in words is a challenge. He is a uniquely multifaceted individual, embodying wisdom, strength, and humility in ways that words alone cannot fully express. Ron is a man of many layers, each contributing to a life of purpose, kindness, and quiet strength. He inspires not through grand gestures, but through the simple yet profound way he lives each day.

Ron's journey, captured in the pages of this book, is a testament to the strength of a life rooted in love and a commitment to seeing the good in all people. It's an honor to share this foreword, and I hope these words convey even a fraction of the incredible, loving individual Ron truly is.

With love and utmost respect,

Louie Rochon
Whidbey Island, Washington

Introduction

Over the past five years, I have written numerous essays under the overarching theme of "Reflections of the Heart!" Each one is a testament to my enduring quest for deeper understanding. These writings reflect my belief that within each of us lies a unique blend of knowledge and wisdom. As I explore various topics, I uncover fresh insights and profound truths — not only about the world but about myself and the essence of what truly matters in life.

Writing, for me, is a journey of learning, self-discovery, and sharing. I seek to weave a tapestry of perspectives, reflecting the rich and many nuances of life. Having written so many essays about life and living, you may find recurring themes that reflect enduring lessons and insights gathered along the way.

This book is a distinctive expression of life's many facets. Shared with an open heart, I offer optimism, insight, and hope, ever mindful that each new day is a gift. A gift I choose to embrace fully, using it to stand for love, compassion, and gratitude.

I do not claim to possess more knowledge or wisdom than anyone else, nor do I aim to teach, change, or convert others. My intention is simply to share my thoughts and beliefs, recognizing that each of us walks a unique path on life's journey. It is my hope that something within these pages will resonate with you, lift your spirit, and make a positive impact on your life.

Respectfully and always with love,

Ron Roesler

1

HOW I SEE MY WORLD

Honoring every Elder's life journey, contributions and wisdom

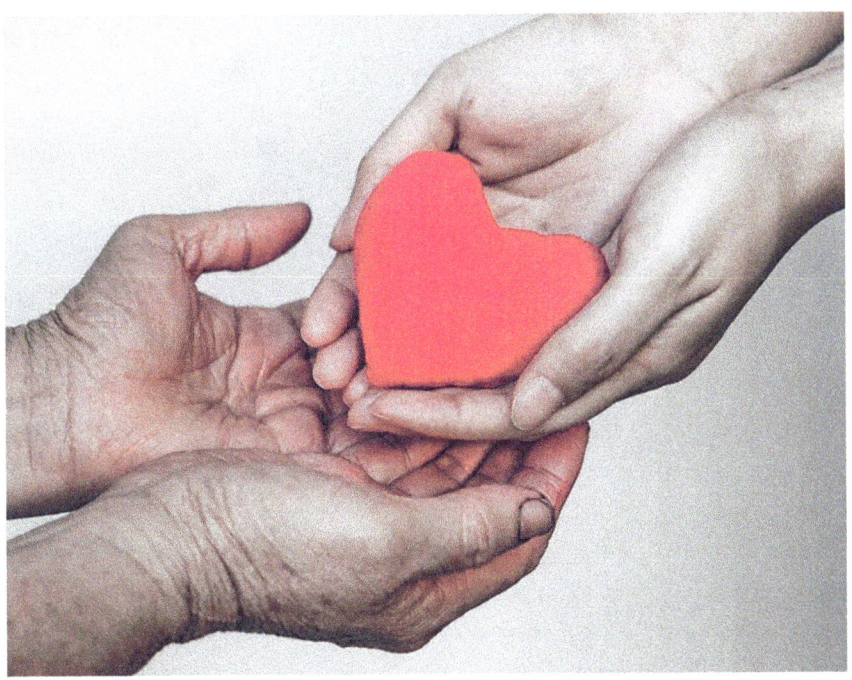

Note: This was my first essay written (updated from April 2020) and shared during the early days of the pandemic to foster connection and hopefully bring light into another "shut-in's life." Much of what is shared here is written in the first person, sharing the journey as my own, without assuming it will resonate with everyone. Take what feels true for you and brightens your life, and leave the rest.

Some forty years ago, I began to understand a truth that would forever shape my life: I am responsible for and create my own reality. Before this shift, I was most often entrenched in a perspective that something was "wrong," with others and the world, or that some ominous event was always around the corner. Unsurprisingly, life most often mirrored back these assumptions. I wouldn't say I walked through life as a dark force, but my thoughts led me down darker roads, steering me away from the fullness of life and joyfulness.

I can't pinpoint precisely what sparked the change, perhaps it was something I read, or I was simply exhausted from wading in pools of negativity. Whatever it was, I consciously chose to turn things around. I began to look for the good in people, to embrace the beauty of life itself — and almost immediately, I noticed how this invited more light, connection and happiness into my world.

One of my associated revelations at the time was that if I desired something more in my life, it was up to me to embody and express it. *"Be the change you wish to see in the world,"* Gandhi's words echo here. So, today when I long for deeper friendships, I now chose to take the first step by being more outgoing and open-hearted. When I desire more love, I strive to cultivate even greater love in myself and share it freely.

Also today, I aspire to support peace, compassion, and love! Not only as concepts but as daily practices. I know the world harbors both light and darkness, yet I choose to see the good, focusing on what is possible rather than dwelling in fear or unfounded projections. As the theologian Thomas Merton put it, *"Our job is to love others without stopping to inquire whether or not they are worthy."* Today, my life is absolutely richer, more fulfilled and joyful.

In fact, I actively steer clear of things that amplify darkness in my mind— violent movies, stories steeped in vengeance or the sensationalism often included with newspapers and TV. Instead, I choose uplifting content that inspires empathy and connection, even shedding a tear for the unusual heartfelt commercial or a light-hearted romantic comedy. I find that by immersing myself in positivity, I receive peace and serenity in return.

Now two months shy of 84, I live with my wife, Helene, in what I consider paradise here on Whidbey Island, just 30 miles Northwest of

Seattle. Despite retiring from 35 years of rigorous racquetball at 78, my passion for life, exercise and connection remain vibrant. I now play golf regularly for the exercise and opportunity to connect with a great bunch of guys, I feel the joy of each day as a blessing, and I'm grateful for the ability to continue pursuing the activities I love.

Retirement, for me, is not an excuse to slow down but a personal invitation to make contributions to others wherever I can. My latter career with Chrysler Corporation was devoted to fostering quality and cost improvements across various organizations. I facilitated transformations within corporate divisions. My journey has been filled with opportunities to achieve positive change. Reflecting on those years, the lessons in respecting others, teamwork, humility, and resilience remain essential guides.

A cornerstone of my career was recognizing the power of asking for ideas from the people doing the work. I firmly believe that *"none of us is as smart as all of us,"* as Ken Blanchard said, and this rings true in every effort I have undertaken. By honoring each individual's insights, we create a path forward together, blending our strengths to achieve collective success.

To me, success is less about personal achievements and accolades and more about cultivating an environment where we all succeed together.

Indeed, I am profoundly grateful for the support I've received along the way, from the many thank-you notes I've received over the years, to the Chrysler Chairman's Award presented to me by Lee Iacocca, and the Presidential Point of Light Award from President George H.W. Bush for community contributions in inner-city Detroit. These recognitions were affirmations of a lifelong commitment to improvement and service — a drive that continues, even as my focus has shifted to writing and sharing my thoughts.

Along the way, one of my most gratifying experiences has been my volunteer work with the ManKind Project (MKP), an organization dedicated to helping men lead lives of integrity and service. As Elder Chair for MKPUSA.org, I was honored to inspire and support elders across the country, fostering a resurgence of purpose and pride in elderhood. Recently, an elder MKP friend wrote to me, saying, *"In you, I see a leader who embodies vision, humility, and the ability to inspire and unite."* Receiving this was a "wow" for me! I am grateful and deeply moved by the impact this work has on me and others and the way it fulfills my own drive to leave a legacy of service.

Amid these successes, I also acknowledge my missteps. As a younger man, I stumbled and made a ton of mistakes — each one a lesson, an opportunity to learn and grow. This series of life reorientations have resulted in a deep sense of gratitude and humility that remain with me today. These experiences have shown me that the path to wisdom is rarely linear but is always valuable.

So, as I look to the future, I am eager to keep contributing, to lend my gifts toward making a positive difference. As Martin Luther King Jr. once said, *"Life's most persistent and urgent question is: What are you doing for others?"* It's not about the prestige; it is about the purpose and joy of knowing that, even in my later years, I am still focused on helping others.

Thank you for allowing me to share a glimpse of my journey, a journey filled with growth, setbacks, discovery, and the enduring drive to give back. May we each find ways to bring light into the world, however small or large our contributions may be, they do make a difference! ♥

Personal Reflections of Your Heart from This Essay

As you reflect on this essay, consider responding somehow to the following question: *What in this essay made a positive difference for you?*

2

A DANCE WITH TIME: THE WISDOM OF ELDERHOOD

A lasting legacy of love, wisdom, and compassion

When I was young, I often imagined the day I would step into the shoes of an adult, believing — as many teenagers do — that I had it all figured out. I wore the cloak of invincibility, certain that my view of the world was complete. But as the sands of time slipped through my fingers, my understanding began to shift.

In the bustling environment of a Chrysler engine plant, I found my voice as a foreman, sharing victories and weekly updates with my team. As my career progressed, my words found their way into the Chrysler Times newsletter, where they sparked conversations on leadership, corporate culture, and the power of continuous improvement.

Time, I've come to realize, is a master illusionist. Thirty years passed in what felt like the blink of an eye. And before I knew it, I was standing at the threshold of elderhood, not as the "smartest" but as one who has discovered the vastness of what remains unknown. This, I believe, is where true wisdom begins to grow.

Being 82 is a brand-new adventure, filled with both reflection and discovery. With longer life expectancies, many of us are navigating the uncharted waters of extended elderhood. My writings now reflect this stage of life, aiming to spark recognition in others on similar journeys.

In life's darkest corners, I've discovered a radiant source of light: gratitude. This simple yet profound perspective has the power to transform an empty glass into one brimming with possibilities. When we pause to count our blessings and savor joyful memories, we are bathed in a sea of thankfulness — for life, for friendships, and for the opportunity to make a meaningful impact.

Elders are uniquely positioned to offer the gift of their wisdom and experiences to future generations. Here in South Whidbey, a community rich in elderhood, I see the profound potential we have to leave a lasting legacy of love, wisdom, and compassion.

Aging, I've found, is far more than a physical process. It brings with it a deep maturity, a serene presence, and a kind of inner grace. In my younger days, I often asked, "What's in it for me?" But with time, my focus shifted. Service replaced self-interest, community replaced isolation, and giving became more important than gathering.

As elders, we embody compassion, humility, and morality, carrying a treasure trove of insights for younger generations. I aspire to be a beacon of moral and spiritual guidance, igniting the flame of inspiration in those around me. As Marcus Aurelius wisely observed, *"Waste no more time arguing about what a good man should be. Be one."*

Writing has become my sanctuary, a canvas on which I paint my reflections and life lessons. It gives me purpose and allows me to share what wisdom I've gained with others.

No matter how many candles are on your birthday cake, the journey of learning and growth never truly ends. Embrace the world with the curiosity of a learner, show compassion, and grow with grace. Be a vessel of humility, morality, and empathy. And always, no matter the circumstances, count your blessings.

Such blessings come in various forms. Recently, I found a new treasure, *The Short Bible: A Chronological Summary of the Old and New Testaments* (Peter Bylsma, WestBow Press, www.shortbible.com). This concise summary deepens our understanding of biblical history and God's eternal plan. Its accessible style has become a guide, helping us see the interconnectedness of life's chapters and the enduring narrative of God's love; the love most deserving of our gratitude.

Gratitude, after all, is the torch that illuminates even the darkest paths. As William Faulkner once said, *"Gratitude is a quality similar to electricity: it must be produced and discharged and used up in order to exist at all."* So, let us light up our lives with gratitude and dance in its radiant glow. ♥

Personal Reflections of Your Heart from This Essay

As you reflect on this essay, consider responding somehow to the following question: *What in this essay did you find most meaningful?*

3

SUBLIMELY GIFTED!

It is in this bold sharing of our true selves that we find our highest calling — to live fully, to love deeply, and to give freely

Have you ever truly considered the depth and variety of the gifts you possess? No matter where we find ourselves in life, each of us has been entrusted with profound God given gifts. First, the gift of life itself — a miraculous, unrepeatable chance to experience, to grow, and to contribute. Each of us has also been endowed with intelligence, a unique blend of talents, and countless opportunities to make a meaningful impact.

In a world often dominated by strife, struggles, and the relentless noise of media sensationalism, there is a deeper spirit within us — a spirit of greatness waiting patiently to be uncovered. It lies just beyond the din of daily life, a quiet yet powerful gift that resides within each of us, waiting to be revealed. This greatness, intrinsic and sacred, is part of who we are.

The person God created in each of us is beyond our imagination. Often, we live only within a small fraction of the potential we were designed to embody. C.S. Lewis once wrote, *"There are no ordinary people. You have never talked to a mere mortal."* Each of us carries an extraordinary essence, placed within us by our Creator. Imagine the possibilities if we fully recognized and embraced this divine origin within ourselves.

Embracing our God-given gifts means living wholeheartedly, with all the unique beauty and strength we've been blessed to embody. It's about seeing ourselves as not just adequate but extraordinary. Opening our minds to this perspective enables us to step into a world brimming with potential and purpose.

Saint Paul's words in Romans 12 speak to the beautiful diversity of our gifts and the call to use them wholeheartedly. He writes: *"Therefore, I urge you, brothers and sisters...do not conform to the pattern of this world but be transformed by the renewing of your mind... We have different gifts according to the grace given to each of us. If your gift is prophesying, then prophesy in accordance with your faith; if it is serving, then serve; if it is teaching, then teach; if it is to encourage, then give encouragement; if it is giving, then give generously; if it is to lead, do it diligently; if it is to show mercy, do it cheerfully."*

Yet, our greatest challenge is often within. We must step beyond our self-imposed limitations and quiet the inner referee, that well-trained critic shaped by a lifetime of fears, past criticisms, and internalized notions of inadequacy. This inner voice, aimed at protecting us, may have prevented us from realizing our potential. Silencing it allows us to show up fully in the world, unhindered by self-doubt.

As Marianne Williamson reminds us, *"Our deepest fear is not that we are inadequate; our deepest fear is that we are powerful beyond measure. It is our light, not our darkness, that most frightens us... Who are you not to be? You are a child of God. Playing small does not serve the world."*

Overcoming fear, reclaiming our greatness, and embodying our true selves is not just an opportunity; it is a calling to step into our true nature. It is about sharing our gifts, contributing to the greater good, and moving out of the self-imposed comfort zones that keep us isolated. It is about having the courage to step forward despite fears, knowing that growth lies on the other side of comfort.

Yes, I have learned over time that stepping beyond comfort carries risks — fear of being wrong, criticism, even rejection. Yet, in staying comfortable, I found that the freedom from criticism came at a cost: the absence of growth, of learning, and the missed chance to make a difference. Playing small, as Williamson so rightly put it, does not serve anyone, least of all ourselves.

So, I choose to continue sharing encouragement and hope, aspiring to make a difference, however small, in the lives of those around me. Each step forward means quieting that inner referee, stepping beyond comfort, and seeing the possibility of goodness and light that awaits.

It's about knowing that God, as our creator, has gifted each of us with many gifts, including his Son Jesus, and loves each of us unconditionally! Give yourself and others the gift of your full, authentic self.

It's about showing up, stepping into courage, and leaving behind the weight of fear.

It's about sharing our gifts with compassion, understanding, and empathy.

It's about growth, learning, and finding purpose, anchoring ourselves in a deeper sense of meaning.

It's about seeking the greater good and making a positive difference in our communities and the world.

It's about sharing your gifts and love fully, without reservation.

In the end, each act of courage, each risk we take to live out our gifts, weaves together a legacy not just of personal growth but of contribution to a better world. As Helen Keller once said, *"Alone we can do so little; together we can do so much."* Let us all step forward, united in purpose, embracing the gifts within, not just for ourselves, but for the beauty, love, and light we bring to the lives of others.

It is in this bold sharing of our true selves that we find our highest calling — to live fully, to love deeply, and to give freely. ❤️

Personal Reflections of Your Heart from This Essay

As you reflect on this essay, consider responding somehow to the following question: *What fears are preventing you from being your full authentic self, and how might you overcome them?*

4

FORGING A MORE MEANINGFUL LIFE!

Deepen your understanding of what feeds your soul

I've been reflecting deeply on what it means to "feed one's soul." After much contemplation, I've come to believe the following elements, among others, have consistently nourished and continue to sustain my soul:

- My partnership with my wife Helène
- God, Spirituality, and Spiritual Growth
- Self-care
- Our many opportunities to connect with others
- Building and honoring relationships
- Creative expression through writing and sharing
- Making a positive difference
- Intellectual stimulation

- Emotional fulfillment
- Continuous learning and growth

At the heart of all of this is my extraordinary partnership and love for Helène. Surrounding that love is our shared belief in God, Spirituality, and the continual pursuit of Spiritual Growth. I am focusing today on these first two elements — Helène and our relationship and our spirituality — though I may address others in the future. Let me be clear: what follows is about us, our choices, and the path we've chosen, which has brought us deep fulfillment, happiness and peace.

No matter what your past holds, exploring and embracing sacred practices can be a guiding light in life. There are as many interpretations of religion and spirituality as there are people, and I honor each person's journey. Ours has been rooted in a lifelong devotion to Christianity, celebrating the birth of Jesus Christ and our belief in God, whose grace has shaped our lives in immeasurable ways.

For me, spiritual growth is about seeking greater meaning and purpose, a journey guided by the belief in something far greater than our physical selves. This search for meaning is not unique to Christianity; it is a universal quest found in all cultures and faiths, offering connection with the divine and a broader perspective on our existence.

Our connection to God is fortified by spiritual practices such as worship, rituals, prayer, and meditation. These practices provide not only a sense of inner peace but also offer a profound way to connect with like-minded people. They invite us to pause, reflect, and embrace gratitude — principles that bring clarity and purpose to our daily lives.

Worship, for example, is more than an act of devotion; it is a bridge between our human experience and the divine. Rituals, whether weekly or personal, offer us the opportunity to engage with life's deeper questions, to feel part of something much larger than ourselves. These sacred acts build the moral and ethical framework that guides both individual and community behavior, helping us align our actions with our values.

Such practices also stir deeper questions about our purpose, our identity, and the legacy we are shaping. Engaging in this introspection is central to our well-being and a key part of leading a fulfilled life. As I reflect on this, I am reminded of the words of C.S. Lewis, who said, *"You don't have a soul. You are a soul. You have a body."* This powerful sentiment captures the essence of spiritual growth, reminding us that the soul is our truest self and must be nurtured and fed for us to live meaningfully.

In seeking a deeper connection with God, I often find solace in scripture. One verse that resonates deeply with me is Matthew 6:33: *"Seek first the kingdom of God and His righteousness, and all these things will be added to you."* It is a reminder that when we place God at the center of our lives, everything else — our hopes, our relationships, our sense of purpose — falls into place.

Believing in a power greater than ourselves, and actively pursuing a life grounded in faith, brings a profound sense of peace, purpose, and belonging. These are not just abstract ideas but are vital ingredients in a life well-lived, sustaining our souls in ways nothing else can.

As we nurture this spiritual foundation, it naturally fosters optimism about the future. Embracing the goodness inherent in all people, recognizing our capacity for personal growth, and holding hope for peace in the world are acts that replenish the spirit and uplift those around us. As Mahatma Gandhi once said, *"Be the change that you wish to see in the world."* These words call us to reflect on our spiritual growth and, in doing so, become forces for good in our communities.

In closing, as we step into the future — wherever that may lead — I encourage you, no matter your beliefs, to embark on your own journey of spiritual growth. Take time to deepen your understanding of what feeds your soul, explore the practices that resonate with you, and embrace the peace and fulfillment that comes from a life connected to something greater. By nurturing your soul, you not only enrich your own life but also inspire others to do the same, fostering a world filled with hope, love, and faith. ♥

Personal Reflections of Your Heart from This Essay

As you reflect on this essay, consider responding somehow to the following question: *What benefits might you experience from spiritual nurturing or connection?*

5

LOVE DEFIES A SIMPLE DEFINITION

I find myself longing for a richer definition of love's true depth

As I reflect on love, I find myself questioning the most common descriptions. What truly lies within the heart and soul of love? It is much like the ocean — we understand its surface and perhaps a few hundred feet below, yet its hidden depths largely remain a mystery.

The dictionary defines love as "an intense feeling of deep affection" or "a deep romantic or sexual attachment." It adds examples like "give her my love" or "with love" as ways we convey warmth. While these definitions touch on aspects of affection, they often miss the profound, soul-deep essence that love embodies. In contrast, the Bible's 1 Corinthians 13:4-5 offers a more layered view: *"Love is patient, love is kind. It does not envy, it does not boast, it is not proud. It does not dishonor others, it is not self- seeking, it is not easily angered, it keeps no record of wrongs."* Here, love is not merely an emotion but a virtue — an active commitment to kindness, humility, and patience.

Yet, even with these beautiful insights, I find myself longing for a richer definition of love's true depth. Beyond fleeting emotions, there is "agape" — the selfless, unconditional love that sustains through every season. Agape love in marriage is what binds a couple and family, nourishing forgiveness, respect, and service, day by day.

My love for Helène is all of these things, and so much more. To me, the dictionary's mention of "sexual attachment" misses the mark; our love is a spiritual connection, one that transcends the physical. When I say, "I love you" to my wife, I reach into the deepest part of my soul, touching something far beyond words. It is a connection not only to her but to God, who lives within each of us.

How else can I describe what has happened to me since falling in love with Helène? She is the stars in my universe, the melody in my heart. She is my symphony, my "Ode to Joy." Her touch brings light to my world, and her embrace is a daily reminder of life's beauty. As Beethoven once said, *"I must despise the world which does not know that music is a higher revelation than all wisdom and philosophy."* Like music, love reveals truths that logic cannot grasp.

When I say, "I love you," I mean that our hearts beat in harmony, resonating with the same universal rhythm. We dance to an inner symphony, one that only grows in depth and beauty as time passes. I promise to always pitch my heart next to hers, attuned to the same key.

Each day, we renew our love with simple gestures — morning kisses, comforting touches, goodnight embraces. Love, I've come to believe, is the quiet devotion we pour into these moments. As poet Elizabeth Barrett Browning wrote, *"I love thee with the breath, smiles, tears, of all my life."*

When I say, "I love you to Helène," I mean that I will be your constant in every storm, offering my truth, my understanding, and my shoulder to lean on. Rain or shine, joy or struggle, I promise to listen and support you with every ounce of my being. In you, I have found a partner not only for life but for eternity. As C.S. Lewis observed, *"Affection is responsible for nine-tenths of whatever solid and durable happiness there is in our lives."*

These days, I see us as a perfect circle — without beginning, without end. We simply are. It is a circle of connection, joy, and discovery, where I am who I am, and she is who she is. In this sacred space, I find love, acceptance, and the unshakeable joy of simply being together.

Helène, even at age 84, with the struggles of aging we face, your laughter, your quirky humor, and your endless creativity continue to light up my life. You bring joy not only to my heart but to everyone you meet. You are still the woman who keeps me laughing and dancing. Thank you for being you and for loving me. You are the essence of joy in my life, and when we are together, I feel we radiate that joy into the world.

You have become part of my very essence, just as I am part of yours. We no longer stand alone, nor would we want to. Who I was before we met has transformed into who I am now — a man whose heart and soul are intertwined with yours. In truth, my love for you defies description, but if I must try, it is this: I love you with all that I am and all that I hope to be. My deepest desire is to spend each day we are given on this earth with you. As the poet Rumi once wrote, *"Lovers don't finally meet somewhere. They're in each other all along."*

Finally, our love is a journey, a timeless dance of souls intertwined. It is the constant promise that, come what may, we will walk hand in hand through every chapter, every sunrise, every sunset. As our lives continue to unfold, I am grateful for each shared moment, each silent understanding, and each expression of our love. Here's to the journey — together, always, without end. ♥

Personal Reflections of Your Heart from This Essay

As you reflect on this essay, consider responding somehow to the following question: *In what ways is love a part of your life?*

6

THE PATH TO BEING MYSELF

It's never too late to consciously tap into the goodness within,
to shine that light into the world.

From my earliest days, I longed to be "grown up" — to emulate those older than myself. In grade school, I would look up to any older child, silently observing, eager to uncover the essence of who they were and how I might emulate them.

I modeled myself after my parents, relatives, teachers, mentors at church, and the older kids in school. Each person I encountered became a piece of my evolving identity. I was learning what it meant to "fit in," adopting styles, approaches, and mannerisms in an effort to create an image that felt "right" to me.

As I look back, I realize I was unconsciously crafting an inventory of traits and behaviors to form my unique self. *"We are what we repeatedly do,"* as Aristotle observed, and in this quiet process, I was building a self- image that reflected those I admired. But in doing so, I also sometimes took on qualities that perhaps veiled my true self.

On a deeper level, I yearned for harmony and connection, without ever really thinking about it, I was hoping to root myself in love, goodwill, and shared values. My intent was always to bond with others on common ground. Yet, in my search for connection, I became a patchwork of influences — some genuine, some influenced by ego and many missteps along the way.

Isn't this true for most of us? Our traits, our quirks, and our inclinations shape who we are today. We each travel a unique path to discover the essence of being grown up. But it raises an important question: have I, or have we, chosen wisely?

So, when people advise me to *"just be yourself,"* I pause. What does that really mean? After all, I am who I am. But how do I connect with my truest self amidst the layers of traits I've adopted over a lifetime? And, in doing so, can I reconcile who I've become with who I was meant to be?

The Bible tells us we are made in God's image — it conveys a pure and perfect starting point. Yet, as the philosopher Søren Kierkegaard said, *"The most common form of despair is not being who you are."* I find myself asking how to reconnect with that divine purity within — how to peel away layers of ego and learned behaviors to reveal the God-source at my core.

I find the heart to be my closest link to authenticity. When I feel uneasy, I know to pause, realign, and ask myself if I am truly speaking from the heart. Often, that unease signals the intrusion of ego. I strive to remain vigilant, checking myself: Am I truly listening to my heart? Am I respecting the presence of others, their perspectives, and their shared humanity?

Over time, I've developed an inner compass of values — integrity, accountability, humility — and they guide me. When I find myself judging, I remember the importance of looking for the good, of focusing on kindness and compassion rather than allowing negativity to cloud my vision. This has been transformative, proving that my perspectives are powerful forces in shaping my/our reality.

It's true: if we want more love, we must be more loving; if we want greater connection, we must offer kindness. Each of us holds the power to shape our world by embodying the very qualities we seek.

Of course, I am far from perfect, especially when facing those with rigid, self-centered attitudes. While I am still learning, I know that remaining heart-centered, choosing to react with patience rather than judgment, is essential to my own peace and growth.

Helène and I have found deep fulfillment living by these principles, sustained by faith and the joy of uplifting one another. Our love and partnership continue to make life joyful and balanced, regardless of the inevitable challenges we experience as we age. Life, I've found, is a rich tapestry when woven from positive intentions, kindness, humility, and shared respect.

In the end, true happiness is not merely about reaching a destination but about becoming. With age, I have come to see that authenticity is not something to attain but a way to be each day, with every choice and every word.

As I reflect on this journey of becoming, I realize that authenticity is a lifelong endeavor, a willingness to align our thoughts and actions with our truest selves. *"This above all: to thine own self be true,"* Shakespeare wrote, urging us to strip away pretense and embody who we truly are. So, here I stand, with gratitude for the wisdom and love gained along the way, embracing the essence of who I am — continually striving, learning, and refining. It's never too late to consciously "be yourself," to tap into the goodness within, and to shine that light into the world. ♥

Personal Reflections of Your Heart from This Essay

As you reflect on this essay, consider responding somehow to the following question: *How are you respecting the presence of others, their perspectives, and their shared humanity?*

7

LIFE'S JOURNEY: THE ANGELS AMONG US

*Never doubt that you are, have been,
and will continue to be an angel to others*

Life's journey is a continuous quest for knowledge, understanding, and growth — an evolution that begins at birth and extends into our elder years. Each stage brings its own unique set of challenges and lessons that shape who we are, weaving together a tapestry of experiences, choices, and personal growth. This learning happens through our interactions with family, friends, educators, clergy, and life partners. These "teachers," whether seen or unseen, become the vital threads in the radiant mosaic of our lives.

I think of these teachers not just as advocates or mentors, but as "angels." They are the ones who have launched us into life and the many lifelong bearers of friendship, guidance, and wisdom. Being open to receiving the wisdom they offer, regardless of our age, is essential for personal growth. *"It is the mark of an educated mind to be able to entertain a thought without accepting it,"* as Aristotle once said. Openness leads to greater understanding, while arrogance only blinds us to the lessons life continually offers.

Our early angels are often our family, gently guiding us through the first steps of life. I think back to my childhood, remembering with deep fondness how my grandparents would pick us up each Sunday during the 1940s to attend church, while my father served in the Navy. These small acts, combined with the warmth of our large family gatherings and my parents' quiet yet profound love, laid the foundation of my values — though many of their lessons only became clear much later in life. Faith in God has been a constant through every phase of my journey, a guiding star that continues to shine today.

As we grow, we encounter other angels who may impact us profoundly, often without our immediate realization. Teachers like Mrs. Reed and Mrs. Petroski, whose warmth, humor, and kindness left an indelible mark on my heart, are examples of this. Their impact reminds me of Maya Angelou's words: *"People will forget what you said, people will forget what you did, but people will never forget how you made them feel."*

In life's journey, it is vital to pause and recognize the angels — those who light up or lighten our path. I have been blessed by many such angels, some of whom are no longer with us, like Elaine, Roger, Lee, Maury, Betty, and Toni, to name a few. And still today, there are more angelic friends, who bring light into my life. One such angel, Bill Elbring, introduced me to the transformational experience of The ManKind Project in 1994. MKP's mission — to foster emotional maturity, spiritual awareness, and community responsibility among men — profoundly changed my life. Through MKP, I've learned the value of integrity, accountability, compassion, and authenticity. Angels like Don Jones, with his quiet humility and deep wisdom, have been my mentors on this journey of personal transformation.

In my professional life, I've also been touched by angels. Marty Allard, a wise elder and one of my colleagues at Chrysler, taught me invaluable lessons that shaped my career. Then there was Christopher Steffen, Chrysler's EVP and Controller, who mentored me through my executive growth. These lessons went far beyond work — they were life lessons that enhanced my interactions with others and helped me see the good in those around me. Indeed, those who see the good in others are angels themselves.

Life's challenges also bring their own lessons. My mid-life crisis at fifty, though painful for my family and friends, ultimately became a period of rebirth. In losing much, I gained clarity, understanding, and the essential gift of self-forgiveness. Through this painful chapter, new angels emerged, guiding me forward with compassion and wisdom.

As we all move through life, we are graced with many angels — offering us friendship, support, and wisdom. It is crucial to remain alert to these blessings, acknowledging and appreciating the unexpected angels who appear in our lives. My beloved wife, Helène, is a shining example of such an angel, and together we navigate the tides of life, constantly being each other's angels.

Whether they are still present or have passed on, the angels we encounter remind us to live with gratitude and love. Never underestimate the importance of recognizing their contributions to your growth and your life's story. And just as importantly, realize that you, too, are an angel in the lives of others. As Mother Teresa once said, *"Not all of us can do great things. But we can do small things with great love."* Every act of kindness, every moment of compassion, contributes to the ripple of good in the world.

Finally, never doubt that you are, have been, and will continue to be an angel to many others. Whether through a random act of kindness, a listening ear, or paying it forward, your actions can illuminate someone's path. Often, simply listening can be the most powerful angelic gift of all.

Personal Reflections of Your Heart from This Essay

As you reflect on this essay, consider responding somehow to the following question: *Who have been the angels in your life and which of their characteristics can you emulate to inspire others?*

8

IMAGINE!

Imagine how spectacular we really are!

No one tells the oceans or the trees
or the mountains that they're too old.
They talk of how powerful, how grounded,
how awesome they are.
Imagine if we thought the same way about ourselves as we got older.
Maybe we'd realize how spectacular we are.

Becky Hemsley

Whatever your age, there is no denying it — we are survivors! Survivors who have been finely honed by the waves of time. Life challenges and teaches each of us, much like the natural forces that shape oceans, trees, and mountains, as depicted in Hemsley's poem. Reaching seventy years of age or more carries a badge of honor, symbolizing not just survival but resilience and grace.

No matter your current age or stage of life, this badge of honor signifies greater wisdom, depth, and discernment. Our responsibility, yours and mine, is to embrace how powerful, grounded, and magnificent we truly are. This journey is about shedding the image of who we were — or who we thought we were — and fully stepping into the reality of who we are today. In essence, it's about releasing the past and embracing the present.

This process is both a challenge and an opportunity for renewal. Imagine if we viewed ourselves with the same reverence as we age as we did in our youth. It's not about what others think; it's about us fully owning our own magnificence. Whether we believe it or not, we are the culmination and epitome of God's creation. *So God created man in His own image, in the image of God He created him; male and female He created them*" (Genesis 1:27). Recognizing this divine imprint reminds us of our shared inherent worth.

As I write, I reflect on a life challenge that has quietly influenced my behavior to this very day. As the eldest of four siblings, I often found myself unfairly held accountable when things went wrong around the house. Though I was frequently innocent, the assumption of my guilt seemed automatic. Now, at almost eighty-four, I recognize a lingering habit that arose from those experiences: defensiveness when confronted. This moment of reflection, however, brings new insight, revealing more about who I am and who I strive to become.

I share this because acknowledging my defensiveness offers me the opportunity to break free from its hold. I am more than the responses shaped by my youth, and perhaps, if we each take time to reflect, we'll realize just how extraordinary we truly are. As the psalmist declares, *"I praise you because I am fearfully and wonderfully made; your works are wonderful, I know that full well"* (Psalm 139:14). Embracing this truth allows us to see beyond our past habits and into the brilliance of our full potential.

With a title of *Imagine*, this would not be complete without a few of John Lennon's famous words:

> *Imagine all the people Livin' life in peace*
> *You may say I'm a dreamer But I'm not the only one*
> *I hope someday you'll join us And the world will be as one.*

Today, in our eighties, we embody the majesty of oceans, mountains, and ancient trees, drawing strength from God, each other, and the friendships we have nurtured. Despite the trials of health, missteps along the way, and the ever-changing world around us, we continue to endure with grace. Though we found each other later in life, our love stands as a testament to the timeless beauty of the human heart. Each day begins and ends with words of love, and we envision a future together, extending into our nineties and beyond. As Scripture reminds us, *"Even to your old age and gray hairs I am he, I am he who will sustain you"* (Isaiah 46:4). Our love reflects this divine promise of enduring care. ♥

Personal Reflections of Your Heart from This Essay

As you reflect on this essay, consider responding somehow to the following question: *What is one of your negative tendencies you could limit en route to a better you?*

9

SEEDS OF GREATNESS

It's about standing in your power and letting your greatness shine.

We are born with the seeds of greatness nestled within our souls — a divine gift from God, quietly awaiting expression. Have you ever truly considered the depth and breadth of how you've been blessed? Despite life's circumstances, the mere gift of existence is something to cherish. Each of us is imbued with intelligence, unique talents, and countless opportunities to manifest our greatness.

The person we are created to be is magnificent beyond mortal comprehension. Yet most of us live within a fraction of our potential, never fully realizing the astonishing being we were designed to become. To claim our God-given talents and express them fully is to live authentically, as the singularly beautiful and beloved individuals we were meant to be. This embrace of our true magnificence opens the doorway to a universe of possibilities.

In St. Paul's words to the Romans, we find the strength to rise beyond conformity: *"Do not conform to the patterns of this world, but be transformed by the renewing of your mind... For we have different gifts according to the grace given to each of us."* Paul encourages us to express those gifts fully — whether in prophecy, service, teaching, encouragement, generosity, leadership, or mercy. It is through this wholehearted expression that we honor God's design.

Our greatest challenge does not lie in our lack of ability but in the self-imposed barriers that constrain us. Past emotional wounds, inner criticism, and fear are formidable opponents. That inner critic, shaped by a lifetime of external judgment, tells us we are inadequate. But silencing that voice allows our unique greatness to shine through, unobstructed.

Remember the words of Marianne Williamson mentioned in essay three (Sublimely Gifted), *"Our deepest fear is not that we are inadequate; our deepest fear is that we are powerful beyond measure.* The call to step through fear and reclaim our true selves is not just an opportunity — it is a sacred responsibility. We are meant to live boldly, sharing our gifts generously, emerging from the shadows of self-doubt, and stepping forward in faith, even when uncertainty looms.

Over the years, I, too, have wrestled with fear — fear of the unknown, fear of failure, fear of standing fully in my power. What if I take this leap? What if I fall short? Yet the wisdom I return to time and time again is this: *"Whether you think you can, or you think you can't — you're right."* (Henry Ford). The battle is often won or lost in the mind before any action is taken.

Staying within the confines of my comfort zone may offer a sense of peace, but it also stifles growth, learning, and the opportunity to make a meaningful impact. Playing small, as Williamson suggests, serves no one. But showing up in our greatness — allowing our light to blaze forth — serves not just ourselves but the world around us. Yes, fear will always accompany us on this journey, but it need not petrify us. We can choose to evolve despite it.

In my desire to make a positive difference, I continue to share these reflections, hoping that in some small way, my words might brighten your path. And still, each time I prepare to send these messages into the world,

I feel the same apprehension. Yet I choose to quiet that inner critic, step beyond the boundaries of comfort, and embrace the potential for good, trusting that authenticity will always resonate.

So, I say to you: Give yourself, and the world, the sacred gift of your full, authentic self.

It's about showing up wholeheartedly.

It's about walking through fear and abandoning the limitations of comfort.

It's about sharing your unique brilliance, not holding it back.

It's about continual growth, deeper learning, and finding an elevated purpose.

It's about seeking the greater good and making a lasting impact.

It's about standing in your power and letting your greatness shine.

And in doing so, you not only transform your own life but also elevate your community and the world. ♥

Personal Reflections of Your Heart from This Essay

As you reflect on this essay, consider responding somehow to the following question: *In what ways can you use your gifts to serve your community?*

10

LIFE'S PATH: SHAPED BY CHOICES AND BELIEFS

Forgiveness paves the way for a life filled with joy. Forgive and Live!

Life is undeniably shaped by the choices we make and the beliefs we hold. As time passes, our decisions — or even our indecisions — create a ripple effect, influencing the course of our personal journeys. What is often over- looked is that our thoughts, not just our actions, play a crucial role in molding our experiences and shaping the world around us. *"For as he thinketh in his heart, so is he"* (Proverbs 23:7). Our thoughts are the seeds from which our reality grows.

It is essential, then, to be mindful of our thoughts, for they are not mere reflections but powerful forces that shape our lives. By cultivating positive, constructive thoughts, we can enhance not only our own well-being but also the lives of those around us. This perspective transcends specific religious or spiritual beliefs — it is a universal truth.

Religion, regardless of the denomination or your personal belief system, offers unique opportunities for growth, connection, and fulfillment. Studies have shown that religious involvement can lead to better health outcomes, including increased longevity. In 2018, *National Geographic* reported that "attending religious services bolsters our immune system and can extend our lifespan." Religious involvement, at its core, invites us into a community where shared values and mutual support foster resilience and joy.

From a Christian perspective, being part of a faith community goes beyond health benefits. It involves experiencing the unconditional love and grace of God through Jesus Christ and embracing the Good News — a message of salvation and eternal life. As 2 Corinthians 5:17 reminds us, *"Therefore, if anyone is in Christ, the new creation has come: The old has gone, the new is here!"* This message, central to Christian teaching, transcends fear and focuses on the abundant life that God offers through faith.

In the early days of Christianity, fear was often used as a tool to keep believers on the 'right' path. Over time, however, there has been a shift — a return to the heart of Jesus' teachings, which emphasize love, inclusion, and freedom of choice. Fear has taken a backseat as churches today increasingly emphasize the positive, life-affirming messages of the Gospel. In this light, Christianity becomes not just a belief system but a way of living that fosters community, love, and mutual support.

Despite the beauty of these teachings, there has been a noticeable decline in church attendance in recent years. This presents a challenge for church leaders. How can they, amidst the demands of daily life and an ever- changing world, continue to nourish their congregations and expand their reach? The answer lies in reimagining what it means to belong to a church community.

Church leaders today must not only honor the timeless truths of the Gospel but also find innovative ways to deepen the spiritual experiences of their congregants. This includes creating vibrant weekly services, but it also means fostering a sense of belonging that transcends Sunday mornings. A strong church community provides members with opportunities for engage- ment, growth, and connection. It creates a space where individuals feel seen, heard, and valued — a spiritual home where love reigns over fear.

For Helène and me, this sense of belonging has been beautifully exemplified at Trinity Lutheran Church on Whidbey Island. The church, led by a humble yet visionary minister, creates an environment where the teachings of Jesus Christ come alive through warmth, inclusivity, and a genuine commitment to the well-being of all. The church is not just a place to attend services; it is a family, a community that offers a sense of purpose and belonging. We have found joy in being a part of something greater than ourselves — a family that shares our values and our faith.

Yet, beyond the walls of any church, the choices we make each day shape the quality of our lives. Life, with all its challenges, losses, and opportunities, is constantly evolving. We have been given the gift of free will — the power to choose how we respond to the ebb and flow of our existence.

Choosing the "low road" of negativity, resentment, or indifference, no matter how justified you believe, will undoubtedly lead to more pain, isolation, and a diminished quality of life. On the other hand, choosing the "high road" — one of love, kindness, and faith — brings not only joy but also a life rich in meaning, connection, and even greater longevity.

Helène and I choose to walk the high road, surrounding ourselves with communities of love, like Trinity Lutheran, and embracing each day as a chance to grow, love, and find joy. As Ralph Waldo Emerson wisely said, 'The only person you are destined to become is the person you decide to be.'

Forgiveness, too, is a profound healer — it opens the door to freedom from pain and paves the way for a life filled with joy, whether we extend it to others or ourselves. Forgive and live!

So, I ask you: How do you visualize the quality of your journey forward? What choices will you make? The path ahead is never set in stone, and it is never too late to choose a brighter, more fulfilling road. Let your thoughts and your choices be the foundation upon which a life of joy and love is built. ♥

Personal Reflections of Your Heart from This Essay

As you reflect on this essay, consider responding somehow to the following question: *What steps can you take to improve your church's (or community's) impact?*

11

"Rocks": Reflections on Stability, Connection, and Endurance

Never doubt that you are a rock for others in your life!

Helène tending our rock garden!

Perhaps you've made it through life without consciously thinking about the role rocks play in our lives. Yet, they are ever-present, both as physical objects and metaphors for things that endure.

Maybe, in your past, like me, you've skipped a few rocks across water, or you've used them in landscaping to add beauty to your surroundings. Some of us even keep rocks as keepsakes — reminders of places, moments, or people we cherish. I keep a sliver of an ancient rock I found in India with my sacred objects as a reminder. For the most part, rocks are long-lasting, seemingly simple inanimate objects. Yet, whether we see them as utilitarian, decorative, or symbolic, rocks are an important part of life!

Allow me to further explain the many uses of rocks. They have become powerful metaphors in our lives. One significant way "rock" is used is to symbolize longevity and resilience. Rocks, by their very nature, are durable and resistant to change. They withstand the elements over vast periods, enduring where most other materials decay or erode. This resilience makes them a symbol of permanence. As Jesus said in the Gospel of Matthew, *"Therefore, everyone who hears these words of mine and puts them into practice is like a wise man who built his house on the rock"* (Matthew 7:24). Building upon a rock represents a solid, unshakable foundation in life.

The Bible refers to God as the "Rock of Ages," a symbol of His eternal strength and protection. The well-known Christian hymn *Rock of Ages*, written in 1762 by the Rev. A.M. Toplady, was inspired by his experience of finding shelter in a rocky crevice during a violent storm. This hymn echoes the idea of God as an unmovable, steadfast force in our lives. Similarly, the phrase "You are my rock," used between life partners and close friends, conveys a sense of stability, emotional support, and strength. It's an acknowledgment that through the storms of life, certain people provide an unshakeable presence — just like God does for those who seek His refuge.

Rocks, however, are not just symbolic of strength — they also represent connection and rhythm. The term "rock and roll," which emerged from African American vernacular in the early 20th century, originally referred to movement and rhythm, particularly in a spiritual sense. By the 1950s, it became synonymous with music that moved the soul, giving rise to great artists like Elvis Presley, The Beatles, Jimi Hendrix, and many more. This movement of rhythm and rock connected generations, much like how the rocks in our personal lives — the people and communities we hold close — ground us through their shared presence.

We often find strength in a community of like-minded individuals who serve as our metaphorical rocks. For us, these foundational "rocks" include God, the love Helène and I share, our immediate family, our church community, my golfing friends and community, and the two remarkable and loving women who support us daily. These cherished relationships provide love, stability, companionship, and a meaningful buffer against loneliness. They are the anchors that offer us love and constant encouragement into the future.

The friendships we cultivate, the family we cherish, and the mentors we trust become the steady pillars that ground us. As the poet John Donne wisely noted, *"No man is an island, entire of itself; every man is a piece of the continent, a part of the main."* In a world where solitude can easily take root, intentionally choosing our community with care is essential to fostering a sense of belonging and preserving our connection to others.

Free will allows each of us to decide which "rocks" play the most significant roles in our lives. Some are foundational — our life partners, the love we embrace, and the beliefs that give us purpose. Others are symbolic — friends, acquaintances, and moments of joy that make life richer. But all contribute to our sense of reality and connection.

Among these rocks, the gemstones of life are often those older than ourselves — those who have lived long enough to offer the wisdom and perspective that only time can bring. They represent the brilliance and refinement that only come through enduring the pressures and challenges of life. As Proverbs 16:31 reminds us, *"Gray hair is a crown of splendor; it is attained in the way of righteousness."* These elders, like polished gems, shine brightly in our lives, adding depth and richness to our own journeys.

Ultimately, I have found that having a rock garden of friends, family, and mentors greatly enriches my life. They are the steady presences that remind me of our shared humanity, resilience, and the importance of enduring love and connection. In a world that is constantly shifting and changing, it is the rocks we each hold onto that give us the stability to move forward with perseverance and grace.

In reflecting on the significance of rocks, both literal and metaphorical, they serve as anchors in a constantly changing world. Whether as symbols of strength, reminders of connection, or sources of wisdom and love, the rocks in our lives are the foundations upon which we build. As we travel the path of life, choose your rocks wisely, recognizing that they hold the power to shape our journey, support us in times of need, and enrich our hearts with lasting meaning. And finally never doubt that you are a rock for others in your life! ♥

Personal Reflections of Your Heart from This Essay

As you reflect on this essay, consider responding somehow to the following question: *Who or what is a rock in your life?*

12

THOUGHTS ON THE PURSUIT OF HAPPINESS

How do we sustain happiness when life inevitably gets in the way?

"Happiness is more than a pursuit; it's a decision."

Our Founding Fathers immortalized these words in the Declaration of Independence, words that Congress refined into their final form:

> *We hold these truths to be self-evident, that all men are created equal, that they are endowed by their Creator with certain unalienable Rights, that among these are Life, Liberty and the pursuit of Happiness.*

Pursuit: "The action of following or chasing someone or something."

Now, consider this — why must happiness be something we pursue, as though it were a prize just out of reach? Why not something we already possess?

While I don't claim the wisdom of our Founding Fathers, I wonder why they didn't assert our right to preserve happiness, rather than pursue it?

Why can't we just be happy? I say we can. Yes, "stuff" happens that disrupts our joy, but life will always present challenges. It's the very nature of life throwing obstacles our way. Still, the key question remains: How do we sustain happiness when life inevitably gets in the way?

The loss of a spouse or life-partner is devastating and a time for grieving. And yet, happiness and grief shape each other, reminding us of the depth of our love. They walk together, hand in hand, allowing us to heal while still finding light along the way. As Kahlil Gibran wrote: *"The deeper that sorrow carves into your being, the more joy you can contain."*

Happiness, in the end, is a choice. Not to diminish the significance of life's trials — some are indeed devastating — but even amidst life's storms, we can choose happiness.

Here are a few lessons I've learned over my eighty-plus years…

The first lesson is that, even in the midst of life's storms, the good things remain. When we pause to reflect, we realize that no matter how severe the storm, life's blessings do not disappear.

Sometimes, we find ourselves feeling low, consumed by the weight of what's happening. Yet, these are the very moments to consciously shift focus, to gratitude, to reflect on the blessings in our lives. This shift allows us to strengthen our resolve and reawaken our joy. Happiness, though interrupted, always finds a way back — if we allow it.

Despite the inevitable struggles, we can steer our lives toward joy. We can choose to dwell on the good, not just in life's circumstances but also in the people around us. It's easy to focus on the negative — both in life and in others — but doing so robs us of our own happiness. Instead, by choosing to see the good, not only do we foster our own joy, but we also open ourselves to deeper connections and friendships.

As Abraham Lincoln once said, *"Most folks are about as happy as they make up their minds to be."* It's a sentiment that has stood the test of time, and one that reminds us of the power of our own perspective.

Finally, we embrace each day as a gift. We live in the present, filled with gratitude, just as Eckhart Tolle advocates in his work, *The Power of Now*. He writes:

> *"The power of now will help balance your life by subduing the thoughts of your past and the future and focusing on the present moment, which itself is the truest path to being happy."*

These life lessons are available to all of us, each day, if we so choose. Life is brief — why not live it with a sense of joy and contentment? Happiness is more than a pursuit; it's a decision.

This gray-haired interpretation of our "unalienable Rights" reframes the pursuit of happiness as the preservation of happiness. Despite life's inevitable challenges, we each have the ongoing right to be happy. ♥

Personal Reflections of Your Heart from This Essay

As you reflect on this essay, consider responding somehow to the following question: *When was the last time you chose happiness in the face of adversity?*

13

THE KID WHO LIVED
DOWN THE BLOCK

A world founded on inclusiveness, compassion, caring, and love.

The kids and I hope this finds you in good health and thriving!

I crafted the "Kid" narrative to highlight what I consider four essential factors for the future health of humanity:

1. Addressing the tragic loss of life, especially the heartbreaking loss of young lives to war, domestic terror, or mass shootings. This represents a profound challenge to our collective human spirit. Each child lost or seeking refuge and is turned away embodies an unrealized promise for contributions to humanity and future generations that may never be realized.

2. Addressing the current hostility and division toward those seeking refuge in the U.S. raises the need for a poignant reminder that no

matter who you are, all of our ancestors were once newcomers in search of a brighter future in The United States! Many went on to achieve unimaginable greatness.

3. Acknowledging whatever our beliefs, God gave each of us seeds of greatness! These seeds can only grow to fruition within an open society with education for all. A society that recognizes and embraces inclusiveness, compassion, caring, and love for all, irrespective of ethnicity, religion, skin color, or life choices, as reflected in our U.S. Constitution.

4. Addressing the paradoxical idiom that global thinking is important and the powerful truth that acting locally underscores local actions as the bedrock of global change. In essence, the state of the world mirrors the strength of our local communities and resolve, or the absence thereof.

These four items are vital for the well-being of the global community and future generations! Thank you for taking the time, and now, "The Kid!"

Seeking refuge, a young foreigner named Alexei and his family immigrated from a faraway country to a small town in America, bringing traditions and stories from a world unknown to us. With his quiet demeanor and keen observations, Alexei quickly became known to us as the bright foreign kid who lived down the block.

Despite his reserved nature, Alexei was bright. His mind was a fertile ground for ideas and dreams. He excelled in school and his intelligence shone through in every subject, but it was in his social studies debates that his passion truly ignited. Inspired by stories of justice and fairness, Alexei wanted to become a lawyer.

Years went by, and Alexei's dedication to his studies never wavered. He attended a prestigious university, excelling in law courses, and eventually became a respected lawyer. His journey didn't stop there. His fairness, empathy, and sharp mind led him to become a judge, a role in which he served with honor and dignity, always striving to ensure justice was well served.

Alexei's journey didn't end in the courtroom. His sense of duty and passion for justice propelled him into the political arena. He became a member of the United States Congress, a position he used to represent his constituents and be a voice of reason for those who couldn't speak for themselves. His colleagues respected him and his constituents loved him for his unwavering commitment to fairness and progress.

But his story is not only a story of success. It's a reflection of what is possible in a world where thousands of young people lose their lives each year to senseless killing. Humanity loses countless possibilities like Alexei's.

Each of these children could have been a doctor, an artist, a humanitarian, a judge, a leader, or a voice for change. Their potential contributions to society, the advancements they could have driven, the lives they could have touched – all lost in the devastating ravages of conflict between unresolved differences.

Alexei's journey from being a foreign kid who kept to himself to becoming a highly respected member of Congress mirrors what humanity can gain when peace prevails. It reminds us that within every child worldwide lies a universe of possibilities, and when we protect and nurture all young lives, we invest in a future of positive advancement for all of humanity.

Every child saved is a potential beacon of hope, a story of what can be achieved when we choose understanding over prejudice, love over hate, or peace over conflict.

"The Kid" story is a beacon of hope, and the following list reflects just a few of thousands of successful refugee stories. Refugees who left the oppression of their home countries and immigrated to America not as criminals but as survivors and ultimately made outstanding contributions to humanity, the U.S., and the world.

Albert Einstein – Country of Origin: Germany.
Reason for Seeking Refuge: Escape from Nazi persecution.
Developed the theory of relativity, significantly impacting the field of theoretical physics, Nobel Prize in Physics in 1921.

Madeleine Albright – Country of Origin: Czechoslovakia.
Seeking Refuge: Political unrest and the threat of communism
First female U.S. Secretary of State, influential in foreign policy.

Elie Wiesel – Country of Origin: Romania Seeking Refuge: Holocaust survivor
Nobel Peace Prize laureate, author of "Night," and activist for human rights.

Sergey Brin – Country of Origin: Soviet Union
Seeking Refuge: Jewish persecution
Co-founder of Google, revolutionizing internet usage and information access.

Gloria Estefan – Country of Origin: Cuba
Seeking Refuge: Cuban Revolution
Grammy Award-winning musician, influential in popularizing Latin music.

Levi Strauss – Country of Origin: Germany
Seeking Refuge: Jewish persecution
Founded Levi Strauss & Co., inventor of blue jeans.

George Soros – Country of Origin: Hungary
Seeking Refuge: Escape from Nazi Occupation
Billionaire financier, philanthropist, and political activist.

Freddie Mercury – Country of Origin: Zanzibar (now Tanzania)
Seeking Refuge: Zanzibar Revolution
Lead vocalist of Queen, influential in the world of rock music.

Iman – Country of Origin: Somalia
Seeking Refuge: Political instability
Supermodel, entrepreneur, and pioneer in cosmetics for women of color.

Alejandro Mayorkas – Country of Origin: Cuba
Seeking Refuge: Cuban Revolution
First Latino and immigrant U.S. Secretary of Homeland Security.

Yet, all of this good is overshadowed by the somber reality of lives cut short. Each young soul killed or the kids not given asylum had the potential to leave an indelible mark on the world. They could have been the innovators who solved longstanding problems, the artists who inspired generations, the leaders who guided us toward a more harmonious future, or the compassionate souls who brought diverse local communities together.

For every young life lost, there is also a family in mourning, a community that suffers, and a nation that loses a part of its future. The impact of premature deaths sadly destroys families and leaves deep psychological scars. The ripple effects of these losses not only hinder the present generation but cast a shadow over the prospects of future generations.

Their loss is not just a tally of statistics but a profound loss of what could have been. This also highlights the incredible resilience and potential of those who overcome great challenges. It's a testament to the power of embracing diversity and allowing every person to reach their full potential.

It also speaks directly to the importance of our US immigration system and its potential value to both the US and immigrants of all backgrounds.

However, this also serves as a stark reminder of the disparities in opportunities across the globe. While many have found a path to success, others are denied the basic safety and education to pursue their dreams. This inequality is further exacerbated in war-torn regions with short-sighted, self-serving, or demented leaders, where the very foundation of thousands of children's futures has already been shattered.

We are all called to consider the broader implications of global conflicts abroad and at home and the importance of peace-building efforts as a crucial investment in humanity's future. This is a call to action for all local, state, national, and international leaders to foster a world where every child, regardless of origin or circumstances, can reach their full potential and create a better world for future generations.

Very few of us have the opportunity to effect on a national or international scale. By the same token, we all have full control over what we do as individuals! Regardless of ethnicity, religion, or life choices, we can each stand as a model for others, enabling all within our local sphere of influence to live peacefully, flourish, and reach their full potential. This speaks directly to the oft-used phrase, "Think Globally, Act Locally." I turn this around to acknowledge that Local Actions Drive Global Reality!

How can we each be more understanding and compassionate toward one another?

In conclusion, as we strive for peace, it is most important to acknowledge the profound impact each of us has in our local communities and each life can have on our shared human journey.

There would be countless more stories of innovation and progress in a world where all people have the opportunity to reach their full potential — a world founded on inclusiveness, compassion, caring, and love. The loss of young lives for any reason and each refugee turned away is a dampening of our shared potential and a loss of our collective future. ♥

Personal Reflections of Your Heart from This Essay

As you reflect on this essay, consider responding somehow to the following question: *Who comes to mind when you think of a successful immigrant, and what obstacles did they overcome to achieve their goals?*

14

WEEDING THE GARDEN OF YOUR HEART

Keep your inner garden tended and let only the good grow.

Whether in landscaping, gardening, or lawn care, the importance of weeding is undeniable. No matter who you are or where you find yourself, weeding is both an annoyance and a necessary part of life. It requires time and deliberate effort, and while weeding allows the good to grow, it often leaves behind sore backs and soiled knees.

Weeding takes intentional work.

Yet, if we leave nature unchecked, weeds will proliferate, eventually choking off the beauty of flowers, shrubs, vegetables, and lawns — yes, all the good stuff!

Similarly, in the garden of our hearts, we have a constant opportunity to clear out the weeds — those negative emotions like resentment, unresolved grief, anger, grudges, bitterness, or self- condemnation. When left unchecked, these emotional weeds choke off the best parts of us — our charisma, our connection, and our love.

Perhaps the hardest part is acknowledging the weeds. Denial keeps us from seeing that we all carry these residual emotions, even when we think we've moved on. The most harmful ones are those that pull us away from our true essence, our inner good.

When we hold on to these emotions, we hurt no one but ourselves. They stifle our ability to live fully and joyfully. And just as another person's negative feelings toward us can't harm us, neither do our emotions affect them — they're *their* weeds to pull, not ours.

I've spent a lifetime clearing unwanted emotions and negative energy, and I'll continue until the day it no longer matters. Weeding is an ongoing process, one that requires vigilance and care.

No matter where you are in life or how old you are, today is an excellent time to pull those personal weeds that are holding you back. What negative feelings, those persistent wounds, are you holding onto?

Personal weeding does require intentional work.

Whether you are religious or not, prayer is always a good place to start. Prayer carries the intention to heal, making room for the God-given goodness within you to flourish.

You might also consider seeking guidance from a trusted source — a minister, a therapist, a life coach, or a close friend. In all cases, listening, being vulnerable, and a willingness to change are crucial for effective weeding and personal growth.

Ask yourself, "What do I want more of in my life?" The answer may reveal where healing is needed and where old wounds need tending.

Be kind to yourself in this process. Forgiveness — of yourself and others — is key. Exercise forgiveness fully. Truly forgive! Whether forgiving yourself or another, the depth and sincerity of genuine forgiveness can transform your life.

In this journey of forgiveness, consider the ancient Hawaiian practice of *Ho'oponopono*, a profoundly healing approach to releasing resentment and pain. Its name means "to set things right," and it follows four simple yet powerful steps:

1. I'm sorry.
2. Please forgive me.
3. Thank you.
4. I love you.

As we age, the urgency of this inner work becomes clear. Yesterday, I was 61; today, I am gratefully 81. Life passes quickly, and there's no better time than now to start weeding. By doing so, you'll find your light shining brighter, and with it, a sense of greater fulfillment, accessibility, and happiness.

As Marcus Aurelius said, *"The happiness of your life depends upon the quality of your thoughts."*

Keep your inner garden tended and let only the good stuff grow. ♥

Personal Reflections of Your Heart from This Essay

As you reflect on this essay, consider responding somehow to the following statement: *Consider a weed you could pull to let your inner garden grow.*

15

MULTIDIMENSIONALITY

We learn from our mistakes, refine our understanding, and become wiser

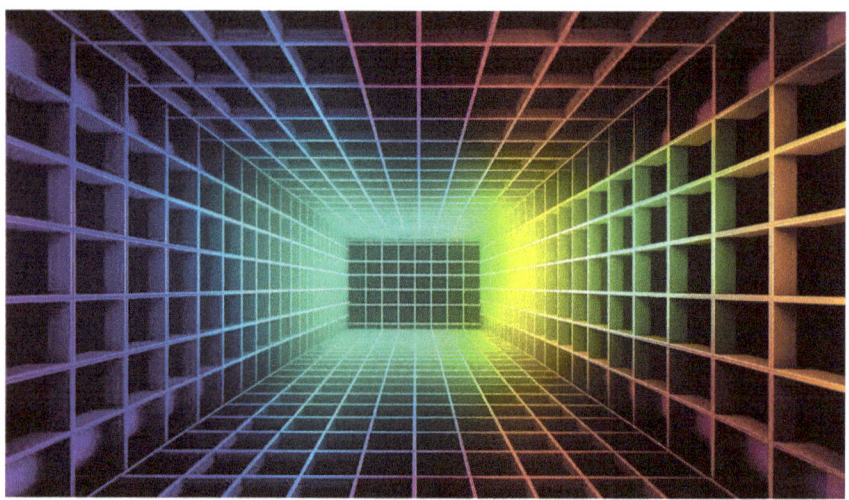

Many years ago, I recall seeing a transparent, multidimensional chess game on Star Trek. Chess itself is already a challenging game for me, and seeing it expanded to multiple levels boggled my mind! I couldn't grasp how an already difficult game, made so much more complex, could be played. Yet, this is what Gene Roddenberry's Star Trek often did — taking us to new, unexplored worlds, both conceptually and technologically.

The thought of multidimensional chess serves as a powerful metaphor for our existence. As multidimensional beings, we are similarly complex, composed of various interests, talents, and layers. We have the capacity to excel in many different areas simultaneously — demonstrating emotional depth, intellectual curiosity, wisdom, and creativity on different levels.

Personal growth experts often describe this multidimensionality in terms of five key areas of development:

- Physical
- Intellectual
- Emotional
- Social
- Spiritual

In the context of God's grand design, we are creators of our unique worlds. With the gift of free will, we actively shape our lives through the choices we make, our responses to circumstances, and the lessons we gather along the way. As the Bible, a timeless source of divine wisdom, says in Micah 6:8 (NIV): *"He has shown you, O mortal, what is good. And what does the Lord require of you? To act justly and to love mercy and to walk humbly with your God."*

Through our decisions and actions, we essentially "create" the path we walk. Whether it is in career, relationships, or the values we hold dear, we continuously construct the reality in which we live. Our choices and experiences are the brushstrokes that paint the canvas of our lives.

Life, as we know, is full of change, challenges, and unforeseen circumstances. How we choose to adapt, learn, and overcome unimaginable difficulties further defines the world we create for ourselves. In this sense, we are not passive observers but active participants in shaping our experiences and, consequently, our lives.

Beyond free will, two of the most profound gifts we have been blessed with are resilience and the capacity for growth. We learn from our mistakes, refine our understanding, and become wiser through life's ups and downs. This continual process of learning and evolving is an integral part of the creative act of living. Every lesson learned and each bit of wisdom gained adds depth and dimension to who we are and the world we shape.

This growth extends beyond the intellectual and emotional; it touches on moral and spiritual dimensions. As we align our choices with higher principles — be it love, justice, integrity, compassion, forgiveness or what we believe — we participate in God's creative work. We are continuously shaping not just our circumstances, but our character and the way we present ourselves to the world.

Although we are all made in God's image, no two people make the same choices, react the same way, or learn the same lessons. Each of our worlds is unique, shaped by free will, experiences, beliefs, and relationships. Consciously or not, this individuality is a reflection of God's image, mirrored through our creativity and choices.

While we are indeed creators of our own lives, we operate within a divinely orchestrated world. Our creative power exists within the framework of God's design. In this sense, we are co- creators, aligning our free will with divine wisdom and growing into the fullness of the image in which we were created.

Yes, we are architects of our unique worlds — making choices, learning from them, navigating challenges, and growing wiser in the process. But this journey is part of a larger divine narrative, where our choices can either harmonize with or deviate from the wisdom and guidance that God offers us.

Thus, while we are each uniquely shaped within God's design, our uniqueness is the result of our own decisions — a true reflection of the freedom given to us by our Creator. Wherever you are in your life, newness and growth are always available!

(As previously noted: "Engaging in spiritual practices, acknowledging and revering a higher power, and connecting with a loving community fosters peace and connection to something greater than oneself. Helène and I are blessed in many ways and draw strength from our belief in God, our church, and our church family. Our life together shines, and our beliefs are crucial to living joyfully!")

"Live Long and Prosper!" ♥

Personal Reflections of Your Heart from This Essay

As you reflect on this essay, consider responding somehow to the following question: *When did you last make a choice that led you one way instead of another and how has that shaped who you've become?*

16

THE POSITIVE RIPPLE EFFECT: WE KNOW IN OUR HEART WHAT IS POSSIBLE

We each contribute to a more understanding and compassionate world!

I believe that, despite life's wounds, an inherent goodness exists in every person. While I may not always like someone, I choose to withhold judgment. After all, with my own imperfections, who am I to judge another? As Wayne Dyer wisely observed, *"When you judge another, you do not define them; you define yourself."*

I strive to highlight the good in life, but when I falter, I acknowledge my own faults and forgive myself. My hope is that we all find the ability within ourselves to embrace others, recognizing that each person bears the weight of life's challenges to varying degrees. By choosing to hold individuals in high regard, I seek and acknowledge the good within them.

Many of us, including myself, carry emotional wounds, often referred to as shadows. Some wounds are so deep that they obscure the light of an individual's goodness. For those who have experienced extreme emotional hardship, these "shadows" can deeply affect how they show up in life. Yet, the pain of another may not always be visible. This truth reminds me of the importance of seeing the inherent goodness in every person, whether their pain is apparent or hidden.

Our response to others should be rooted in understanding, compassion, empathy, forgiveness, and love. After all, who am I to offer anything less? As Martin Luther King Jr. wisely said, *"Causing harm to others not only wounds them but also weighs heavily on the one inflicting the harm."* By consciously choosing to see the good in others, we contribute to a more understanding and compassionate world, reinforcing virtues with each interaction.

In essence, it's about choosing to see and encourage the good in ourselves and others. My hope is that we can all find it in our hearts to welcome everyone, understanding that each of us is a unique reflection of God, as well as a reflection of life's harsher realities. As the Bible reminds us in Philippians: *"Whatever is true, whatever is honorable, whatever is just, whatever is pure, whatever is lovely, whatever is commendable, if there is any excellence, if there is anything worthy of praise, think about these things."*

Amidst the constant flood of challenging news and life's struggles, it takes each of us to reinforce the positivity that we know in our hearts is possible. This point is illustrated by a 2023 National Geographic article discussing the work of Yale University professor Becca Levy, who found that people with a positive outlook on aging live, on average, seven and a half years longer than those with a more pessimistic view. This shows that by embracing positivity, we not only improve our quality of life but extend it as well.

Amidst life's constant flow of opportunities, we also face its inevitable challenges. Yet, within these challenges lies a profound gift: the opportunity to learn and grow. From my experience, few qualities are as universally vital as resilience — the ability to "get back in the saddle." While often easier said than done, this ability consistently tests our mettle.

Resilience draws on fortitude, hope, faith, and wisdom, guiding us through life's unrelenting trials. No one is exempt. Consistently getting back in the saddle reveals a depth of character that defines true strength.

When we face failure — in love, business, relationships, or even a game of golf — it is essential not to lose hope. Instead, shake off the setback and keep moving forward. Lest that seem too simplistic, consider these powerful examples:

- Walt Disney was fired from the Kansas City Star because he "lacked imagination and had no good ideas."
- Thomas Edison's teachers told him he was too stupid to learn. Yet, he went on to hold more than 1,000 U.S. patents and invented the electric lamp, the phonograph, and the movie camera.
- Dr. Seuss had his first book rejected by 27 publishers before selling over 600 million books.
- Michael Jordan was cut from his high school basketball team.
- Abraham Lincoln, born into poverty, twice failed in business, suffered a nervous breakdown, and lost eight consecutive elections. Yet today, he is revered as one of America's greatest presidents.

These stories remind us that success often follows failure. The real mistake is not in being knocked down but in failing to rise again. As Vince Lombardi famously said, *"It's not whether you get knocked down, it's whether you get up."*

For me, faith in God strengthens my resolve to rise again. Belief in a higher power offers a divine partnership and a source of hope for the journey ahead. This belief transcends any specific religion; it is about embracing something greater than oneself. Indeed, 88% of the world's population acknowledges the importance of believing in a higher power.

Now in our 80s, Helène and I count ourselves blessed in many ways, drawing daily strength from our faith in God. Together, we navigate life's challenges with a sense of peace and joy.

Resilience, coupled with faith, has been the bedrock of our life together. It empowers us to live joyfully, even amidst life's harshest realities.

Everyone faces loss, professional setbacks, aging, health issues, and unforeseen hardships. Resilience helps preserve our well-being and happiness, even under the weight of such difficulties. Those who emerge stronger often do so with greater wisdom and a renewed sense of purpose.

Interestingly, golf has been one of my greatest teachers in resilience. I've hit some great shots and some terrible shots on the course, but one of the most important lessons is to shake the bad shots off and approach the next shot with confidence and positivity.

Personal growth is a lifelong journey — whether in knowledge, skills, character, or wisdom. Ultimately, it's about becoming a better version of ourselves. As we grow, we not only improve our own lives but also find a deeper sense of purpose, build self-awareness, and bolster self- esteem.

Through resilience and personal growth, we gain the mastery to achieve our goals, whether they involve career success, artistic achievement, or personal fulfillment. As Helen Keller wisely said, *"Character cannot be developed in ease and quiet. Only through experience of trial and suffering can the soul be strengthened, ambition inspired, and success achieved."*

Helène and I have found that our faith in God provides a partnership and peace of mind that allows us to navigate life's turbulent waters with joy. It is the foundation upon which we build our resilience, and it serves as the source of our strength, hope, and love. ♥

Personal Reflections of Your Heart from This Essay

As you reflect on this essay, consider responding somehow to the following question: *When, in your daily life, do opportunities to see the best in others appear?*

17

HUMILITY

The Quiet Strength of the Soul

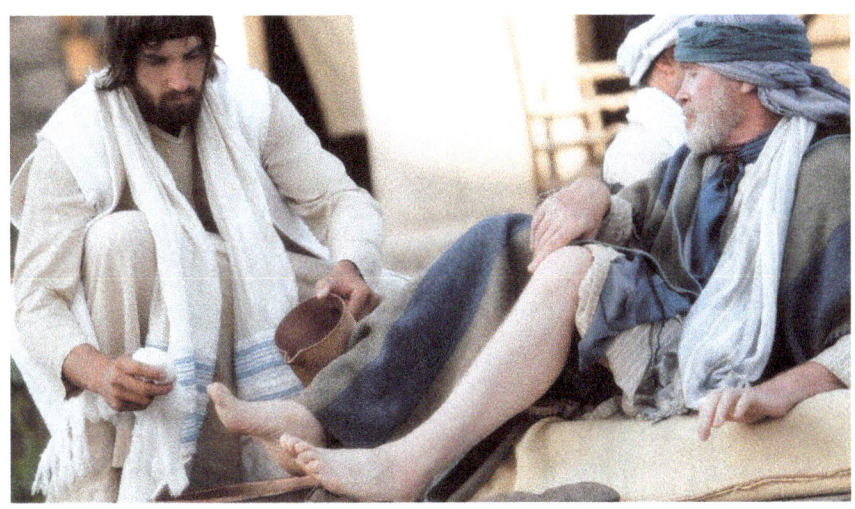

"Humility is a virtue of the highest order!" This sentiment resonates through the ages, and rightly so. Saint Augustine famously declared humility as the foundation of all virtues, reminding us that without it, no other virtue can firmly stand. It's a cornerstone for authentic relationships, encouraging us to value others while keeping our own limitations in perspective. The Bible itself repeatedly calls for humility, a trait deeply esteemed by God and essential for a righteous life.

Humility is not about diminishing oneself or self-deprecation. Rather, it is an honest acknowledgment of our strengths with grace and dignity, while also recognizing our shared human fallibility. It's the opposite of arrogance, which traps us in the small world of the ego. At its core, humility allows us to balance our innate potential for greatness with the ability to admit our imperfections.

C.S. Lewis poignantly observed, *"Humility is not thinking less of yourself; it's thinking of yourself less."* This wisdom reminds us that humility isn't about reducing our self-worth but rather about shifting the focus away from self-centered concerns and toward something greater: serving others.

Understanding our vulnerabilities fosters compassion. When we see our own faults clearly, we become more forgiving of ourselves and others, knowing that mistakes are part of the human experience. Humility deepens our sense of interconnectedness, grounding us in the reality that we are all part of a larger community, bound together by our shared struggles and joys.

A challenge for me, as I reflect on this virtue, is keeping my ego in check. I carry with me the weight of many past accomplishments in church activities, corporate leadership, and community service. My ego often tempts me to recount these achievements as if they alone define my worth.

Yet, I am constantly reminded that others, too, have achieved great things — much greater than my own. True humility involves honoring these achievements without seeking praise, knowing that our worth is not in recognition but in the quiet satisfaction of a life well lived.

In a world often driven by competition and self-promotion, humility is the counterbalance we need. It opens the door to deeper, more meaningful connections and to a life that is enriched not by accolades, but by the quiet confidence of a humble heart. As poet T.S. Eliot said, *"The only wisdom we can hope to acquire is the wisdom of humility: humility is endless."* By embracing humility, we step into a wellspring of strength, wisdom, and peace.

"Intellectual humility" also invites us to a lifelong pursuit of deeper knowledge, truth, and understanding. It is a posture that helps us avoid rash decisions and fallacious beliefs, allowing us to engage with others constructively. Adam Grant, in a May 2024 INC. magazine article, wisely noted, *"Intellectual humility fosters a growth mindset, encouraging us to see challenges and opposition as opportunities for learning rather than threats. Engaging respectfully with opposing viewpoints builds bridges and fosters a culture of learning and collaboration."*

Scripture aligns humility with wisdom. As James 3:13 affirms, *"Who is wise and understanding among you? Let them show it by their good life, by deeds done in the humility that comes from wisdom."* Wisdom does not boast; it is revealed in humble actions, lived out quietly but powerfully.

The path of humility is not easy, but it is transformative. It enriches our lives and the lives of those around us. It strengthens relationships, enables us to honor others, and nurtures compassion. By walking the path of humility with grace and sincerity, we not only enhance our own lives but also extend the gift of humility to all whom we encounter. As we journey together, may we continually remember that true strength lies not in self-glorification but in seeing the good in others — and in ourselves — with eyes of humility. ❤️

Personal Reflections of Your Heart from This Essay

As you reflect on this essay, consider responding somehow to the following question: *In what way can you be more humble without belittling your strengths?*

18

THE WISDOM AND POWER OF FORGIVENESS

Forgive and Live!

Forgiveness is a profound act of strength and wisdom, capable of transforming lives and healing deep wounds. It liberates the soul, bringing peace and reconciliation not only to the one offering forgiveness but also to the one receiving it. At its core, forgiveness holds the power to release us from the chains of negativity, hatred, and hostility, clearing the path toward a healthier and more fulfilling life.

Choosing to forgive is an intentional decision, a courageous act of releasing feelings of resentment and vengeance. It is not about erasing the wrongs or condoning harmful behavior; rather, it is about freeing oneself from the burden of bitterness and anger. Holding onto grudges leads to psychological and physical distress, often manifesting as stress, anxiety, depression, and even serious ailments like high blood pressure and heart disease. As Jesus teaches in Matthew 6:14-15, forgiving others is essential to receiving God's forgiveness: *"For if you forgive other people when they sin against you, your heavenly Father will also forgive you."*

To harbor unforgiveness is to harm oneself, much like drinking poison and expecting the other person to suffer. This wisdom is echoed in many traditions, including the ancient Hawaiian practice of Ho'oponopono, which teaches that holding onto negativity inflicts more damage on the holder than on others. The refusal to forgive, whether others or ourselves, becomes a self- imposed prison of guilt, shame, and mental anguish.

Forgiveness, on the other hand, has the power to heal and transform. It grants us the ability to move forward with greater freedom and joy. Studies show that those who forgive experience reduced stress, improved heart health, and an increase in overall happiness. In forgiving, we also open ourselves to healthier relationships and more enriching experiences. Desmond Tutu, whose work for peace and reconciliation helped heal a divided nation, reminds us, *"Forgiveness says you are given another chance to make a new beginning."*

Helène and I find immense spiritual strength in our faith in God and the power of prayer. Through prayer, hope always emerges, and often, circumstances change for the better. Praying for those who have wronged us is a powerful step in the process of forgiveness. It softens the heart, opens the door to reconciliation, and can even shift the course of events. As James 5:16 affirms, 'The prayer of a righteous person is powerful and effective.' The ancient practice of Ho'oponopono — repeating the words 'I'm sorry. Please forgive me. Thank you. I love you' — fosters inner peace and spreads a ripple effect of healing outward.

If we seek to actualize forgiveness and self-forgiveness, several key steps may guide us:

1. **Empathize**: Try to see the situation from the perspective of the other person, or reflect on your own actions with compassion.
2. **Release Resentment and Self-Blame**: Consciously decide to let go of anger and resentment through prayer, meditation, or speaking with someone you trust.
3. **Focus on the Present**: Shift your attention to activities that bring you joy, fulfillment, and meaning.

4. **Practice Self-Compassion**: Show yourself the same kindness and understanding you would offer to a friend.

Forgiveness heals not only our individual lives but also our relationships, strengthening our communities and that fosters a more compassionate world. As Mahatma Gandhi observed, *"The weak can never forgive. Forgiveness is the attribute of the strong."* In embracing forgiveness, we are helping to cultivate a culture of deeper understanding and empathy. True forgiveness may require courage, but it leads to profound freedom, joy, and new possibilities. As biblical teachings reveal, forgiving others and ourselves yields spiritual, psychological, and physical benefits that ripple through our lives. Indeed, forgiveness offers us a path to live more fully: 'Forgive and Live!' ♥

Personal Reflections of Your Heart from This Essay

As you reflect on this essay, consider responding somehow to the following question: *When in your life have you truly forgiven someone, or yourself, and how did that make you feel?*

19

CHAMPIONS OF THE HUMAN SPIRIT

Seeing the Gold in Others

In a world that often rushes to judge and magnify flaws, the ability to focus on the positive traits in others is a valuable gift. Recognizing the "gold" in everyone we meet opens up a world of uplifting possibilities — not only for those we encounter but for ourselves as well.

At the heart of this practice lies a profound belief in every person's inherent worth. It's about seeing beyond superficial impressions to recognize the goodness, strengths, and talents that reside within. This approach benefits not only our personal relationships but also professional interactions, where identifying and nurturing potential can lead to extraordinary partnerships and success.

Psychological studies consistently demonstrate that people are more likely to rise to the occasion when positive expectations are set. Our perceptions, when grounded in optimism, have a ripple effect: they enhance the abilities of those around us, affirming their value and inspiring them to be their best selves. As we lift others, we too are elevated. Booker T. Washington wisely said, *"If you want to lift yourself, lift someone else."* This simple act of seeing and acknowledging others' strengths also builds our self-esteem, promoting a more optimistic and fulfilling life.

Recognizing the "gold" in others fosters trust and strengthens bonds. It creates a supportive environment where people feel valued, respected, and understood. This is crucial not only in personal relationships but also in team settings, where diverse skills and personalities must align to achieve common goals. Leaders who focus on each team member's unique strengths build harmonious and resilient teams, capable of overcoming challenges together.

Championing the human spirit cultivates a culture of open-mindedness, mutual respect, and empathy. As Ralph Waldo Emerson reminds us, *"Our chief want is someone who will inspire us to be what we know we could be."* When we see the potential in others, we become that source of inspiration. We empower individuals to reach heights they may not have believed possible, fostering a sense of belonging and purpose.

However, this shift in perspective begins with a conscious effort. It requires setting aside judgments, suspending preconceived notions, and approaching each interaction with openness and curiosity. Active listening becomes a vital tool in this endeavor, allowing us to uncover the hidden strengths that others may not even see in themselves. By doing so, we dismantle stereotypes, reduce biases, and build more inclusive and equitable communities where everyone's intrinsic value is acknowledged.

It's essential to note that recognizing the "gold" in others is not about ignoring their flaws or pretending imperfections don't exist. Instead, it's about choosing to focus on the positive, nurturing the goodness that each person possesses. This mindset honors the human spirit and encourages growth. A simple gesture — a kind word, a thoughtful compliment — can unlock this potential and remind others of their value.

As the Bible frequently teaches, we are called to love, honor, and uplift one another. *"Therefore encourage one another and build each other up, just as in fact you are doing"* (1 Thessalonians 5:11). These timeless words remind us that our actions can have a profound impact on those around us, fostering a spirit of kindness and cooperation.

The benefits of seeking the gold in others are immense. By consistently choosing to see the good, we not only enrich our own lives but also create a ripple effect that spreads positivity and understanding. Each day presents countless opportunities to be a "Champion of the Human Spirit." Take a moment today to acknowledge someone's unique worth and let them know you appreciate them, just as they are. In doing so, you contribute to a world where every person's intrinsic value is seen and celebrated. ♥

Personal Reflections of Your Heart from This Essay

As you reflect on this essay, consider responding somehow to the following question: *How has "seeing the gold" in others changed your perspective or positively impacted those around you?*

20

SURVIVING LONELINESS

Caring people are always waiting for you to show up

In addition to claiming millions of lives, the pandemic intensified an already pressing issue in the United States: loneliness, especially among seniors. Loneliness has emerged as more than an emotional struggle — it's a public health crisis. Consider the alarming insight shared by U.S. Surgeon General Dr. Vivek Murthy: *"Loneliness is as deadly as smoking 15 cigarettes a day and more lethal than consuming six alcoholic drinks a day. It is more dangerous for health than obesity."*

Pulitzer Prize-winning journalist Nicholas Kristof also remarked, *"Loneliness crushes the soul, but does far more damage than that. It is linked to strokes, heart disease, dementia, inflammation, and suicide; loneliness literally breaks the heart."*

Antidotes: Feeding One's Soul. Feeding one's soul greatly reduces the adverse effects of loneliness. A study conducted by Brigham Young University analyzed data from 148 studies involving 308,849 participants and concluded that social connections increase an individual's survival odds by as much as 50%. The antidote, then, may lie in caring for, honoring, and nurturing both yourself and others — engaging in what speaks deeply to the soul, beyond material satisfaction or fleeting pleasures.

Feeding one's soul means discovering what resonates at a deeper level — something that enables us to feel more alive, connected, and true to ourselves. This is not merely a survival tactic but a path to a fulfilling, growth-oriented journey of inner awakening.

Engaging in activities that provide emotional, intellectual, and spiritual nourishment is key, particularly for seniors seeking greater meaning and connection in their lives. Here are eleven soul-feeding practices to consider:

1. **Reading and Reflecting on Thoughtful or Spiritual Texts**: Literature exploring life's ethical questions or spiritual teachings can open the mind, inspire reflection, and nurture the soul. Reading thoughtful texts can offer deeper perspectives and promote a profound understanding of ourselves and the world.

2. **Practicing Gratitude**: Gratitude focuses the mind on abundance rather than lack, enhancing overall happiness and satisfaction. The habit of recognizing the positive aspects of life lifts the spirit and helps to counter the weight of loneliness.

3. **Building Relationships**: Meaningful connections are the foundation of human happiness. Building relationships through shared experiences, conversations, or acts of kindness creates a supportive community, forming bonds that stave off loneliness and foster mutual care.

4. **Religious Practices**: Engaging in religious practices offers a sense of peace, purpose, and connection to God. Attending worship services and engaging in religious rituals bring comfort, reduce loneliness, and provide spiritual nourishment.

5. **Contributing to Others**: Volunteering or helping others offers profound fulfillment. As Albert Schweitzer said, *"The only ones among you who will be really happy are those who will have sought and found how to serve."*

6. **Creative Expression**: Engaging in creative outlets such as painting, writing, or photography offers emotional release and a way to process life's experiences. Creativity brings joy and meaning, fostering a deeper sense of connection to oneself and others.

7. **Writing**: Whether journaling, crafting narratives, or expressing personal thoughts., writing is a powerful way to heal, reflect, and discover oneself. It facilitates emotional exploration and offers a meaningful outlet for expression.

8. **Nature and the Outdoors**: Spending time in nature, whether hiking, strolling through a park, or sitting by the ocean, fosters a connection to the larger world. Nature offers rejuvenation, peace, and a sense of belonging to something much greater.

9. **Learning and Growth**: Lifelong learning feeds the intellectual side of the soul. Whether through reading, taking classes, or exploring new ideas, the pursuit of knowledge expands our understanding and strengthens our capacity for resilience.

10. **Mindfulness and Self-Care**: Practices like meditation, yoga, or simply dedicating time to oneself promote emotional well-being. These practices support mental clarity and resilience, reducing stress and enhancing emotional intelligence.

11. **Physical Wellness**: Regular physical activity, whether through exercise or gentle movement like yoga, positively impacts both physical and mental health. Exercise releases endorphins, improving mood and promoting overall well-being.

Each of these practices contributes to feeding the soul, fostering personal enrichment, stronger interpersonal connections, and, most importantly, helping to combat the devastating effects of loneliness.

As poet John Donne once wrote, *"No man is an island, entire of itself; every man is a piece of the continent, a part of the main."*

Remember, no matter your past, caring people are always waiting for you to show up. Take that step — towards them and for yourself. ♥

Personal Reflections of Your Heart from This Essay

As you reflect on this essay, consider responding somehow to the following question: *Who in your daily life may suffer from loneliness, and what actions can you take to ease their struggle?*

21

THE WISDOM OF OPENNESS, LESSONS, AND FRIENDSHIPS

True friends provide safe havens for authenticity, celebrate triumphs with joy

An open mindset toward personal growth and true friendship are among life's most precious gifts. At their core, these gifts nurture bonds that transcend surface connections, delving into realms of mutual understanding, trust, and unconditional acceptance. This profound outlook allows us to embrace every encounter with others and experience as purposeful opportunities for self-discovery and evolution.

Those with an open perspective recognize that the challenges we face — whether from partners, acquaintances, strangers, or personal setbacks — are not obstacles but catalysts for spreading joy. These experiences cultivate invaluable qualities like patience, resilience, and a broader way of thinking. By seeing every situation through the lens of growth, we develop a deep gratitude for the people and circumstances that shape us into our best selves.

Our lives take on new depth, no longer defined merely by events but by the wisdom gained through them. Each day becomes an opportunity to actively learn, grow, and evolve. In this light, challenges are transformed into opportunities, and setbacks serve as sparks for personal transformation. With an open heart and mind, each day becomes an illuminating adventure of discovery, where even the simplest experiences hold lessons. As we adopt this mindset, a shift occurs within us, fostering a deeper sense of peace and fulfillment.

Friendship, too, exemplifies this mindset, acting as a beacon of light through life's ebbs and flows. True friends provide safe havens for authenticity, celebrate triumphs with joy, and offer solace in moments of darkness. Built on foundations of mutual respect, these bonds encourage growth by broadening perspectives and deepening our understanding of ourselves and others.

Moreover, healthy friendships are a balanced dance of giving, receiving, understanding, and compromise. They forge unbreakable bonds that transcend boundaries, offering an unparalleled sense of belonging and purpose. As C.S. Lewis once said, *"Friendship is born at that moment when one person says to another, 'What! You too? I thought I was the only one.'"* These connections, anchored in shared understanding, provide a richness that material pursuits simply cannot match.

In a world increasingly dominated by fleeting interactions and rapid global change, the essence of true friendship and an openness to personal growth become timeless treasures, grounding us in the profound beauty of human connection. These are the rare gifts that enrich our journey, granting us newfound gratitude, deeper wisdom, and an infinite wellspring of joy.

As Albert Schweitzer wisely noted, *"In everyone's life, at some time, our inner fire goes out. It is then burst into flame by an encounter with another human being."*

True friendship and openness kindle that inner fire, fueling our growth and lifting our spirits.

As always, you can take it on to fully experience the profound gifts of Openness, Lessons, and Friendship — or not. The choice is yours. ♥

Personal Reflections of Your Heart from This Essay

As you reflect on this essay, consider responding somehow to the following question: *Who do you consider a true friend and how was the bond between you formed?*

22

TEARS OF UNITY: A CALL FOR COMPASSION, HOPE, AND GLOBAL ACTION

*Perhaps tears are a divine message urging us to
reassess our priorities and values*

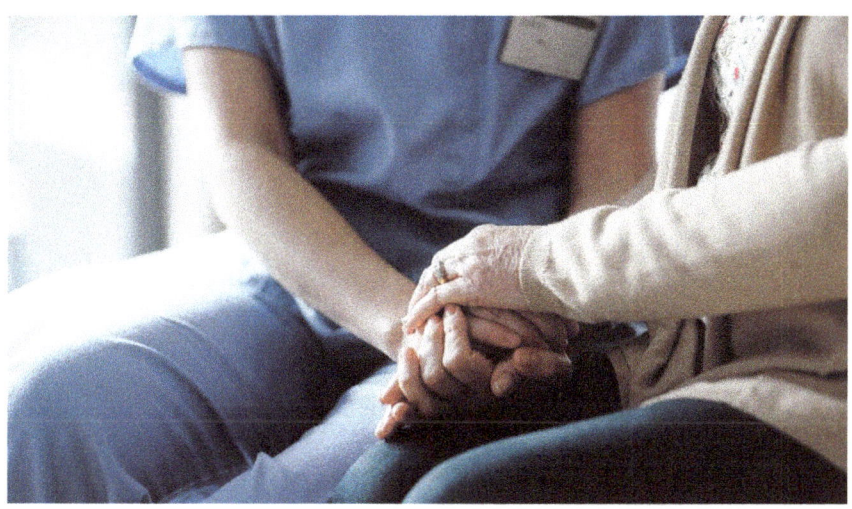

Acknowledging, by all accounts, my seemingly insignificant role in the grand scheme of things, I approach this message with a sense of humility, yet I am compelled to share its importance. I recall a line from a previous article, "Our Thoughts Are Our Reality," which emphasizes that life is about choices. Even in the face of global events beyond our control, we always have the power to choose our personal response.

Recently, a phenomenon in Mexico has captured widespread attention: a statue of the Virgin Mary reportedly shedding tears. Amidst global crises like wars, climate change, resource depletion, gun violence, and political unrest, this occurrence appears as a poignant symbol of humanity's collective struggles.

Perhaps these tears represent our shared grief, or perhaps they are a divine message urging us to reassess our priorities and values. Throughout history, God's mandate to "Love your neighbor as yourself" (Mark 12:31) has resonated not only within Christianity but across many world religions. Eminent philosophers and leaders alike have advocated for compassion, kindness, and love as guiding principles. These teachings call us to active service — to extend love, grace, and support to those in need, thus helping to create a more just and compassionate society.

Despite the wisdom of these teachings, humanity's response has been inconsistent at best. This raises a vital question: What will it take for us to fully embrace and address these timeless messages of love and unity?

While we have made remarkable strides in many significant fields such as biology, medicine, astronomy, physics, and technology, our progress toward global unity, moral integrity, and climate lag far behind. To me, the weeping statue is not just a curiosity; it could well be a divine call to action. Could the following also be considered an example of Divine interaction? It has recently been reported that male fertility rates are declining, a trend that is affecting global population growth. At the very least, a subtle reminder of the fragility of human life.

These challenges point to the urgent need for a global alliance dedicated to urging us to reassess our global priorities, including values, unity, peace, and justice. Yet, our world leaders have not successfully steered us toward such an evolution of heart and spirit. It is time for humanity, our global leadership to chart a dynamic new path forward.

This is where my call to action begins. I believe we must take responsibility for reinforcing peace and unity while addressing these global challenges. Though I feel ill-equipped for such a monumental task, I am convinced that raising awareness and inspiring action is the least I can do.

So, what practical steps can we take? Are there universal commonalities beyond the shared human quest for survival?

Is it possible:

- To unite countries, cultures, and beliefs that seem so different?
- To develop a comprehensive understanding of the State of the World and Humanity, accounting for the many challenges we face today?

- To communicate with leaders globally, fostering cooperation toward a New Worldwide Alliance centered on survival and peace?
- To create an inclusive approach that transcends the goals of the United Nations and individual Countries, recognizing and respecting both our differences and commonalities while fostering dialogue and healing?

Education must play a central role, focusing on moral, cultural, and ethical development. We need to cultivate a global citizenship, grounded in sustainable practices and mutual respect. Our aim should be to foster unity, not hostility. Achieving such a goal will require policy changes, educational reforms, technological innovations, and cultural shifts.

This calls for a united effort from leaders, governments, world religions, international organizations, and communities at all levels — and perhaps in reverse order, starting from the grassroots.

Although my role may be small, I firmly believe in the power of individual influence. Whether through work, service, volunteering, or contributions, each of us has the capacity to make a positive difference. Margaret Mead's words come to mind: *"Never doubt that a small group of thoughtful, committed citizens can change the world. Indeed, it's the only thing that ever has."* This truth holds, even when the challenges before us seem insurmountable.

Though I do not have direct access to global leaders, I share the concerns voiced by King Charles III at COP28, where he called for "genuine transformational action" on climate change. His words resonate with me beyond just that one issue; they speak to the broader need for comprehensive global reform.

As we enter this season of joyful celebration, I pray that we do so with a renewed sense of hope. May the future bring forth new ways to foster global understanding, compassion, and unity. While I sure do not have the answers, I invite your thoughts and suggestions. Perhaps together, we can chart a path toward "genuine transformative action," and in doing so, make a meaningful impact on our world. ♥

Personal Reflections of Your Heart from This Essay

As you reflect on this essay, consider responding somehow to the following question: *In what ways can you promote peace, whether locally or globally?*

23

WEAVING OUR LIFE STORY: THE POWER OF THOUGHTS, FAITH, AND GRATITUDE

Our beliefs mold our behavior and control how we interact with others

The reality is clear: our life's path is shaped by our thoughts and beliefs, which in turn guide our decisions and behaviors. Time flows forward, and the choices we make leave a lasting mark on the story of our lives. It is essential to recognize the pivotal role our thoughts and beliefs play in crafting our reality. Our thoughts are the architects of our inner world, shaping how we experience life and influencing every action we take.

The mind is incredibly powerful — *"As a man thinketh in his heart, so is he"* (Proverbs 23:7). This biblical wisdom captures the essence of how our thoughts define our reality. Emotions like sadness, anger, or fear, when harbored, inevitably manifest in our actions and relationships, often isolating us or leading us into defeat and loneliness. Living in fear can create walls that separate us from others, and immersing ourselves in the tragedies of the world or the sensationalism of media often fosters a sense of hopelessness. When we negatively compare ourselves to others, we deny our own unique worth, and in judging others harshly, we only diminish ourselves. But when we choose to see the good in others, we reveal the goodness also within ourselves.

When I sit down to craft my messages, I carefully select each word to mirror my thoughts and reflect the light I hope to share. My goal is simple: to inspire, uplift, and offer hope. Words, for me, are tools for casting light into the world, and I devote significant time to ensure that my language is clear, precise, and sincere. These are not just words — they are expressions of my heart, shared with the hope that they may uplift someone, even if it is only one person.

As an optimist, I am aware that my perspective could be seen as naïve or dismissive of life's very real challenges. Yet, I intentionally focus on life's brighter side, not to ignore its struggles, but because I believe in the power of hope. *"Faith is the substance of things hoped for, the evidence of things not seen"* (Hebrews 11:1). In my writing, I choose to be a beacon of that hope, especially for those enduring personal difficulties. My desire is that my words, even in their simplicity, will offer comfort, strength, or encouragement to someone — perhaps even to you.

Our choices, whether conscious or subconscious, profoundly shape the direction of our lives. While we may not control every circumstance, we always have the power to choose our response. Life is full of moments where we must decide how we will act or react. By choosing love, kindness, and forgiveness, we align ourselves with a higher purpose. By choosing bitterness or resentment, we allow negativity to erode our spirit. *"Do not be overcome by evil, but overcome evil with good"* (Romans 12:21). In every situation, we hold the power to decide whether we will respond with grace or with resistance.

From a spiritual standpoint, no matter your age or religious background, finding an inclusive, uplifting faith-based community can be one of the most rewarding decisions you make. In such a community, you will discover support, friendship, and a sense of belonging — gifts that grow deeper as you journey through life. Many churches today focus on the inherent goodness of humanity and the transformative power of faith in God, Jesus Christ, and the Gospel. Faith, coupled with positive life principles, lights the way to a joyful, fulfilling life.

Helène and I have chosen to live by a simple yet profound truth: "Gratitude is the light that pierces the darkest of circumstances; living in gratitude is living in that light" This belief has become the foundation of our daily life. Gratitude shifts our focus to the abundance that surrounds us. In the face of health challenges associated with aging, by living in gratitude, we see the countless ways in which we are blessed — often in ways we may have previously overlooked.

In the grand tapestry of life, it is our thoughts, beliefs, and actions that weave the threads of our story. Though time moves forward, and life offers its challenges, we always have the power to choose how we respond. By embracing gratitude, nurturing hope, and sharing love, we illuminate not only our own path but also the paths of those around us. *"Faith is to believe what you do not see; the reward of this faith is to see what you believe"* (Saint Augustine). Let us walk forward in faith, hope, and gratitude, trusting that in doing so, we contribute to a world filled with light, peace, and possibility for all. ♥

Personal Reflections of Your Heart from This Essay

As you reflect on this essay, consider responding somehow to the following question: *Are you part of an uplifting community and, if not, where can you go in your community to become part of one?*

24

THE SACRED ACT OF CAREGIVING

A journey of compassion, love, and service

Beyond our individual pursuits, the true essence of human existence lies in the compassion, understanding, and mutual support that weave the fabric of our shared humanity. At the heart of this connection is the profound role of caregiving — a universal reflection of our innate desire to uplift one another. Caregiving, whether for the ailing, the elderly, or anyone in need, serves as a mirror to the broader human capacity for love and compassion.

While the term "caregiver" is often associated with those who provide direct, intensive care to someone in need, the spirit of caregiving transcends the boundaries of formal roles. Compassion, empathy, and selflessness are qualities we all possess that can be drawn upon throughout our lives. In its purest form, caregiving is an expression of our shared humanity.

Caregiving is not merely about attending to another's physical or mental needs — it is a profound testament to our ability to empathize and express our love. Whether it is a professional caregiver, a family member, or a devoted spouse, caregivers often set aside their own comforts, ambitions, and sometimes even dreams to ensure another's life is more comfortable, joyful, and fulfilled. In doing so, they teach us all the immeasurable value of selflessness.

More than providing assistance, caregivers offer companionship, emotional support, and, often, a hand to hold during life's darkest hours. Caregiving speaks to our deep-seated human need for connection and understanding. As the late poet Maya Angelou once said, *"People will forget what you said, people will forget what you did, but people will never forget how you made them feel."* Caregivers embody this truth by reminding us that true care is not merely about action but about love and connection.

Helène and I are blessed to have two remarkable and loving caregivers, Aimee and Monica who we love and hold as our daughters. They love us and are here daily during the week and Sunday.

From a Christian perspective, caregiving is deeply rooted in the teachings of Jesus Christ, who embodied compassion, love, and service. The Bible offers a powerful reminder of our shared responsibility to care for one another: *"Carry each other's burdens, and in this way, you will fulfill the law of Christ"* (Galatians 6:2). Christ's life exemplified this principle, urging us to love our neighbors as ourselves and to serve with humility and grace. While not everyone is a "caregiver" in the formal sense, the call to serve and care for others is universal, a reflection of God's love manifest in our everyday lives.

Yet, it is vital to recognize the challenges faced by caregivers, especially those who care for a spouse. The emotional and physical demands can be overwhelming, and spousal caregivers, in particular, may feel the strain of isolation and fatigue.

From a personal perspective, the intimacy of the relationship deepens the caregiving experience, but it also heightens the potential for burnout. It is essential to support these caregivers — ensuring they have the respite, emotional outlets, and community connections needed to sustain their well- being. As Proverbs 17:22 reminds us, *"A cheerful heart is good medicine,"* and this truth applies equally to the caregiver and the cared-for. Caregivers must nurture their own emotional and physical health to continue offering the best care possible.

Spousal caregivers are especially at risk of exhaustion due to the close nature of their relationships. Taking time for personal pursuits, staying connected with others in similar situations, and seeking outside support are vital steps in maintaining balance. These connections foster a sense of community and remind caregivers that they are not alone. In caring for themselves, they remain better equipped to care for their loved ones. As C.S. Lewis wisely noted, *"Humility is not thinking less of yourself, it's thinking of yourself less."* This sentiment speaks to the balance caregivers must strike — selflessly giving while not neglecting their own well-being.

On a personal note, after a fulfilling career and numerous executive leadership roles, I now see my role as caregiver for my wife, Helène, as the most meaningful and important role of my life. In our eighties, I treasure each day we share as a gift from God. We have never been closer, and our love, expressed in both small and profound ways, is a constant source of joy. To see Helène's continued happiness is the greatest reward I could ever ask for.

By supporting caregiving and valuing caregivers, we nurture a world where compassion, understanding, and mutual support thrive. This is not merely a societal obligation but a sacred calling — a call to connect with, care for, and cherish the bonds that make us human. In the words of Mother Teresa, *"It is not how much we do, but how much love we put into the doing."* When we embrace the essence of caregiving, we elevate our own lives and those of the people around us.

At some point in our lives, we all become caregivers for one another. Whether we care for an ailing spouse, support a friend in need, or extend a kind word to a stranger, caregiving is woven into the fabric of our lives. In these acts of care, we find the true meaning of our existence.

Helène and I host a monthly Caregivers Meeting at Trinity Lutheran Church in Freeland, WA, on the third Tuesday of each month from 10 a.m. to noon. This gathering offers caregivers a chance to connect, share their experiences, and find support in a community of understanding hearts. All are welcome.

In the end, caregiving is not just a role or duty — it is a sacred expression of love and humanity. It reminds us that the true measure of a life well-lived is not found in personal achievements, but in the depth of our compassion and our willingness to care for others. Whether through small acts of kindness or the devoted care of a loved one, we participate in the ongoing story of human connection. By embracing the sacred practice of caregiving, we cultivate a world where love, empathy, and selflessness reign, leaving behind a legacy that transcends time and touches the heart of what it means to be a caring person. ♥

Personal Reflections of Your Heart from This Essay

As you reflect on this essay, consider responding somehow to the following statement and question: *In some ways, we are all caregivers. Who in your life is a caregiver, and how can you convey your gratitude for their service?*

25

JUST ONE MORE DAY

Or, hopefully, many more!

Imagine having the power to grant an aging soul not only one more day of existence but also the promise of many more filled with golden possibilities. This thought stirs my heart with empathy as it touches on the deepest desire to give hope and connection to those who need it most, and perhaps ourselves. Yet, as we peer behind the veil of our busy lives, we find many elders, and perhaps even younger ones, are quietly tethered to the reality of loneliness.

Loneliness steals the vibrancy from the golden years that should shimmer with love, tender bonds, accumulated wisdom, and treasured memories. But here's the truth we often overlook: we all have the power to make a positive difference in someone's life — whether they are family, friends, or even casual acquaintances. Opportunities to extend a hand, share a kind word, or simply listen are everywhere, and they are far more powerful than we may realize.

As noted earlier, the profound impact of loneliness was laid bare. It crushes the soul and is linked to many types of ailments. It breaks the heart literally and figuratively and can be as deadly as smoking 15 cigarettes a day and consuming six alcoholic drinks a day. I's even more hazardous to health than obesity. In contrast, 148 studies found that social connections boost an individual's survival odds by nearly 50%.

The absence of meaningful relationships and heartfelt interactions creates a silent epidemic of isolation, casting a prolonged and chilling shadow over many hearts. But here's the beautiful truth: each of us possesses the capacity to be a beacon of light for another. We don't need magical powers to combat loneliness; we simply need to reach out with empathy and care.

Daily life offers an endless array of chances to connect — each encounter is an opportunity to touch a heart. Whether in the warmth of our homes, the familiarity of our book clubs, the camaraderie of church gatherings, or even casual conversations at the bank or local store, each interaction holds the potential to dismantle the barriers of solitude. Every smile, every shared moment, every genuine expression of concern can lift the fog of loneliness and restore the warmth of human connection.

Within each of us lies a simple but profound ability: the power of authentic connection. By extending a hand, offering a listening ear, or expressing sincere empathy, we create ripples of hope. In doing so, we are not just brightening someone's day; we are extending the possibility of many more fulfilling days to come. As the Bible reminds us, *"Let each of you look not only to his own interests, but also to the interests of others"* (Philippians 2:4). Through this lens of service, our acts of kindness become lifelines to those who are adrift in loneliness.

Consider the small investment of time it takes to reach out — it pales in comparison to the immense return. A single act of kindness may seem insignificant, but its impact can be life-changing. Every day presents us with new opportunities to break the silence that grips so many. In moments of quiet reflection, I am reminded of the words of Mother Teresa: *"Loneliness and the feeling of being unwanted is the most terrible poverty."* And yet, by simply showing up for someone, we can alleviate that poverty.

For Helène and me, each day is a gift, a chance to brighten someone else's world. We've found that even the smallest gestures of kindness are always well-received, and in lifting others, we too are uplifted. This simple truth holds: "the more we give, the more we receive." The investment is small, the reward is boundless.

As you go about your day, ask yourself: do you know someone who may be lonely? Someone who could use just one more day of hope and connection? Don't hesitate. Reach out, offer friendship, and be that spark of light in their life. You have nothing to lose — and both you and they have everything to gain.

The essence of human connection is simple but profound. Just one more day of genuine care can offer not only hope but also healing. In reaching out to others, we extend the lifeline of belonging, dismantling the walls of loneliness one heartfelt interaction at a time. Let us all commit to using the time we have, today and every day, to brighten the lives of others. In doing so, we breathe life into the words of Proverbs 17:17: *"A friend loves at all times, and a brother is born for a time of adversity."* ❤️

Personal Reflections of Your Heart from This Essay

As you reflect on this essay, consider responding somehow to the following question: *What is one thing you can do to let someone know you see them and care about their well-being?*

26
MASCULINITY AND LOVE

Love transcends gender or societal expectations

Night after night, Helène and I delight in the charm and warmth of romantic comedies. These have become more than just entertainment — they are a nightly ritual, offering us moments of connection and reflection.

From humorous adventures, unexpected encounters, love proclamations to sorrowful separations and emotional reconciliations, these movies conjure up a wave of emotions that resonate deep within us. They invariably lead to a cascade of tears with loving joy every night!

In a world that often labels crying as a sign of weakness, I embrace my tears. To me, they are not a reflection of fragility but a testament to my humanity, an emblem of my romantic nature, and the depth of my heart. As a sentimental soul, I am drawn to these often predictable narratives.

Their depiction of love's challenges, followed by eventual triumphs, touches a core part of me that relishes the beauty of resolution. My tears, far from diminishing me, allow me to celebrate my vitality.

This all led me to ponder the deeper reasons for my emotional responses. Viewed through the lens of an admittedly novice psychologist, yet grounded in my 30 years of experience with the ManKind Project (MKPUSA.org). At MKP, men are taught to become warriors. Warriors of the heart! We learn that true strength is not in repressing emotions but in facing them. Yet, throughout history, men have been conditioned to wear a rugged exterior, to project an image of toughness.

Society, whether implicitly or explicitly, instructs men to mask their emotions, except perhaps for anger. Anger has long been accepted as a "manly" emotion, yet, ironically, it can also be a sign of unresolved pain or fear. Persistent anger is not strength but rather evidence of festering emotional wounds left unaddressed. Beneath this anger often lies fear, the most primal of human emotions, usually buried by a façade of ego and toughness.

These habits of male behavior are reinforced in various ways — by fathers and mothers, peers, and the harsh social conditioning of youth, where vulnerability is often mocked. This lifelong suppression of emotion shapes many men into beings disconnected from their true feelings. But I've learned that true courage lies in embracing all aspects of the emotional spectrum. As author Brené Brown so aptly put it, *"Vulnerability is not winning or losing; it's having the courage to show up and be seen when we have no control over the outcome."*

Love, I believe, is often misunderstood. It is frequently viewed through the narrow lens of family — the domain of spouses, partners, and immediate relatives. Yet, love can and should extend far beyond these boundaries.

For men, however, expressing love in a broader sense often takes on a different form. In male fellowship, love is rarely articulated in words; instead, it is disguised as friendly taunts, playful competitiveness, or the universal fist bump. These seemingly trivial gestures carry the weight of unspoken affection. Louis Armstrong captured this in his timeless song,

"What a Wonderful World," when he sang, "I see friends shaking hands, saying, 'How do you do?' They're really saying, 'I love you.'"

Love is, after all, the essence of our shared humanity. And God's Word emphasizes this repeatedly. In Romans 13:8 (NIV), we are reminded, *"Owe no one anything, except to love each other, for the one who loves another has fulfilled the law."* Love is not optional — it is a commandment. We are called to love one another, not just in the intimate confines of marriage or family, but in every interaction.

As I reflect on my own journey, I carry both heartaches and treasured memories. Remorse for lost friends and loves mingles with the awe of newfound relationships. There are moments when I am wistful for the paths not taken, especially when I see couples who have enjoyed long, loving marriages. Yet, I recognize that each decision, each twist in my life's journey, has led me to where I am today. And it has brought me the greatest gift of all — the deep and abiding love I share with my incredible wife, Helène.

Our nightly ritual of watching romantic comedies is more than a lighthearted indulgence. These stories of love and redemption remind me daily of the bond Helène and I share, of the respect, admiration, and cheerleading we offer one another. Through the joys and challenges of life, we are each other's strongest advocates. In these moments, I am reminded that love, real love, requires vulnerability. It demands that we allow ourselves to feel deeply and express those emotions freely.

As men, we often hide behind outdated notions of masculinity. We downplay our emotions, convinced that indifference is strength. But I've learned that it is in our openness, our willingness to feel and express love, that truly demonstrate strength. When we allow ourselves to be vulnerable, we don't weaken our masculinity; we expand it. In doing so, we embody a fuller, richer humanity, one rooted in love, emotional intelligence, and courage.

And finally, a discussion on love would be incomplete without acknowledging the importance of respecting and valuing our partners as they are. Love is not about attempting to change our spouse; it is about seeing them in their entirety, recognizing their beauty, and celebrating it.

Respect is the foundation of true love, for as 1 Corinthians 13:4-5 reminds us, *"Love is patient, love is kind. It does not envy, it does not boast, it is not proud. It does not dishonor others, it is not self-seeking, it is not easily angered, it keeps no record of wrongs."*

In the end, love is a universal longing, one that transcends gender or societal expectations. Helène and I continue to be each other's cheerleaders, applauding and encouraging one another. Our life together is a gift, and every night, as we laugh, cry, and feel through these romantic comedies, we are reminded of just how blessed we are. ♥

Personal Reflections of Your Heart from This Essay

As you reflect on this essay, consider responding somehow to the following question: *When, if ever, has a movie made you tear up or cry, and what was it specifically about the scene that touched your heart?*

27

THE ILLUSIONARY GUISE OF A PANJANDRUM

Ego skews vision, leading us to gaze upon others
through a self-imposed lens of superiority

In the tapestry of life, we sometimes assume the role of what may be called a "Panjandrum" — a self-fashioned figure of great importance, imbued with an inflated sense of authority and influence.

This illusion, however, often proves to be a clever fabrication of the ego, a veil that distracts us from the depths of our true selves. It is easy to become ensnared by this illusion, as I too have struggled with the allure of self-grandeur. Like a chameleon, the ego transforms, cloaking itself in certainty and luring us from the simplicity and authenticity of who we truly are.

In reality, the only genuine authority we possess lies within ourselves — over our own thoughts, actions, and choices. While this truth may sound elementary, our human tendency skews our vision, leading us to gaze upon others through a self-imposed lens of superiority, which can subtly and harmfully color our perceptions. *"Judge not, that ye be not judged,"* as Jesus reminds us in Matthew 7:1-5, offering a call to humility and self- awareness. His wisdom invites us first to examine our own shortcomings before casting judgment on others, lest we fall into the trap of self- righteousness — a habit that diminishes both ourselves and those we critique.

Instead of falling prey to judgment and conceit, let us choose a path illuminated by respect for the diversity, beauty, and spirit that reside in every individual. By recognizing and celebrating the unique virtues and strengths in others, we also affirm our own worth and humanity. As Maya Angelou so wisely stated, *"We are more alike, my friends, than we are unalike,"* a sentiment that encourages us to embrace the mosaic of differences in roots, beliefs, appearances, and choices that make us whole.

In practicing non-judgment, we cultivate inclusivity, deepen our understanding, and grow in our capacity to accept one another's uniqueness. At our core, beyond our surface differences, we all carry emotional wounds and burdens; we all seek love, purpose, and understanding; and we all yearn for companionship, validation, and the courage to transform our fears into hopes. These shared aspirations remind us of our common humanity and the universal need for compassion.

Life's brevity brings urgency to our choice to become beacons of positive light, acknowledging and uplifting the inherent goodness in each person, especially those who have endured loss, heartache, or profound suffering. It calls upon us to forgive — both others and ourselves — and release the weight of past grievances. This act of forgiveness is a conscious decision to free ourselves from the grasp of the ego, from slipping into the pitfalls of self-importance, or from any inclination toward self-righteousness or sanctimony.

Instead, let us greet each day and one another with open hearts, rejoicing in and expressing gratitude for the light and goodness each of us contributes to the world. As we count our blessings, we strengthen our own resilience and affirm our unique place in the fabric of humanity. Gratitude, after all, is the light that can pierce even the darkest moments; to live in gratitude is to embrace that light and let it guide us forward. ❤️

Personal Reflections of Your Heart from This Essay

As you reflect on this essay, consider responding somehow to the following question: *When have you played the part of the Panjandrum, and how have you since grown to understand the importance of humility?*

28

FINDING MEANING - RECLAIMING DIGNITY

Life's rhythm shifts from the pursuits of building and achieving to the blessings of reflection and giving

At every stage of life, we hold the keys to cultivating health, happiness, and resilience.

Memorializing Love on Puget Sound with Loved Ones!
Ages 90, 86, 82, 90, 81

The first four essential keys — Caring, Compassion, Forgiveness, and Gratitude — are foundational, guiding us to deeper fulfillment and joy. Each key encourages us to reflect and renew.

1. Caring for yourself and others fosters a sense of belonging and purpose.
2. Compassion for both yourself and others invites healing and under- standing.
3. Forgiveness liberates the heart, making room for peace.

4. Gratitude transforms our daily experience, opening our hearts to the blessings in every moment.

As we age, life's rhythm shifts from the pursuits of building and achieving to the blessings of reflection and giving. In this phase, often marked by wisdom, our lives are tapestries woven from the threads of career, family, friendships, losses, and moments of joy and sorrow. The experiences we carry — accomplishments, challenges, heartaches — become touchstones for dignity and self-worth, "a crown of glory," as Proverbs 16:31 reminds us, in the lives we lead.

Historically, retirement implied withdrawal from relevance, but today, with more people reaching into their 80s and beyond, this notion is transforming. Elders possess unmatched experience, insight, and wisdom — a profound resource to themselves and their communities. Each transition, each loss, each reinvention shapes us, yet memories remain, holding life's richest treasures, as Leo Tolstoy wrote, *"Our whole life is but a memory of the better part of ourselves."* When we embrace our stories as lessons, even sorrows become opportunities for growth.

So, the question arises: Do we cling to outdated models of aging, or do we reimagine elderhood as a period of continued relevance, purpose, and joy? Many elders today engage actively, contributing through their unique gifts, embodying purpose in new ways that deepen their spiritual and intellectual journeys. The call is not to rest on past laurels but to continue making an impact, to add meaning and kindness, one choice at a time.

As you envision your life at this stage, ask yourself: What picture would I paint for this season? Shape it boldly. What kind of legacy will you leave, and how will you enrich the lives of those around you?

Living Longer Than Ever

Today's extended life expectancy presents opportunities and challenges. The average life expectancy in the United States is now in the high 70s, and increasing numbers of people are living into their 80s and 90s. In the words of Archbishop Vincenzo Paglia, aging represents "one of the great challenges of the 21st century," urging us to redefine aging with dignity and respect. Pope Francis himself, at 85, recently spoke about the importance of seeing elderhood as a sacred, respected phase, demanding a more compassionate view of our elders.

Aging and Transitions: The Toll and the Triumph

The journey of aging, often marked by role transitions, can strip away familiar identities and bring us face-to-face with questions of purpose: Why am I here? Who cares? This struggle, intensified by isolation and loneliness, was further amplified during the COVID-19 pandemic. Loneliness becomes a thief, stealing joy, zest for life, and dignity, while also becoming a poignant reminder to chart a new vision. Create a future that excites you — no matter your age, your ability to choose remains.

On the flip side, loneliness can drive seniors to despair. Suicide among seniors is an alarming reality, with statistics revealing higher suicide rates among those 65 and older. In 2017, seniors accounted for nearly 20% of suicides in the U.S., according to the CDC, underscoring the profound need for connection, purpose, and compassion.

What We Can Do to Support Elders

Each of us has the power to bring light into the lives of elders in our communities. By fostering meaningful connections, creating opportunities for engagement, and honoring their stories, we affirm the value of their lives and contributions. Imagine the impact of honoring a different elder each month in your church, sharing their life stories, their wisdom, and their advice with the congregation.

Beyond formal gatherings, your presence and friendship can profoundly uplift an elder's life. If you're a senior yourself, seize the opportunity to "pay it forward." Invite a neighbor to dinner, find a group to play cards with, or simply share a coffee and conversation. It's a double win: not only do you offer companionship and joy, but you also rekindle your own sense of purpose, transforming simple acts into meaningful lifelines.

Living with Caring and Compassion

At the heart of it, aging gracefully is about embracing the keys of Caring and Compassion. This timeless call resonates through all cultures and faiths, reminding us that, as Albert Schweitzer beautifully put it, *"The purpose of human life is to serve, and to show compassion and the will to help others."*

Let us honor our elders and ourselves by carrying forward this spirit of kindness and connection. By doing so, we not only give meaning to our later years but also create a legacy of love and dignity that transcends age. ♥

Personal Reflections of Your Heart from This Essay

As you reflect on this essay, consider responding somehow to the following question: *What life lessons have you learned and who might you share them with?*

29

A Cause For Celebration

Embrace each new day as your reason for celebration!

Yes, if you are reading this, regardless of your age or circumstances, you have a cause to celebrate! Each day serves as a reminder of life's fragility, a truth that becomes even clearer as we grow older. Tragically, some younger lives are called to their heavenly home too soon, which only deepens our appreciation for the gift of each new day we are given to experience and cherish.

In our age, Helène and I cherish each day we have together. We see every day as a precious gift from God, and this perspective shapes our lives. Each morning, we greet each other with love, deeply grateful for the blessing of another day to share. Every moment offers a chance to express gratitude, deepen our connection, and live with joy. Our love for God and for one another guides us through each day — truly, all reasons for celebration!

As we age, life becomes ever more precious and uncertain. We come to value relationships, love, and faith over material possessions. This shift reflects not only the passage of time but the deepening of our bond with God. Though we have always been practicing Christians, our connection with Him feels more profound than ever before. As the Psalmist says, *"Teach us to number our days, that we may gain a heart of wisdom"* (Psalm 90:12).

Whatever challenges you face or however dark the days may seem, there is always reason to celebrate. We, too, have felt the deep pain of loss and the heartache of saying goodbye to cherished friends and family. Yet, in those moments of despair, our connection to our Creator has sustained us, offering hope for the future. We endure with strength and gratitude, holding onto the precious gift of togetherness and embracing each new day with faith and anticipation.

It's natural to feel that our darkest moments are uniquely unbearable, and for some, those moments challenge the will to carry on. Yet, that is precisely when we must lean on a power greater than ourselves. As Jesus said, *"Come to me, all you who are weary and burdened, and I will give you rest"* (Matthew 11:28). Immersing ourselves in God's love provides respite from both our and the world's struggles, offering each of us refuge from distress.

These reflections come from a place of profound experience — with adversity, loss, and serious health challenges. These are not the musings of someone untouched by life's hardships. No one reaches old age without enduring trials and there are no free passes!

There are times when I've wondered what drives me to write and share my thoughts. One strong possibility comes from a period between 2004 and 2014, when I lost consciousness more than 125 times. During those episodes, I would fall, unable to brace myself and hit the ground like a dropped sack of potatoes.

During that period, I made multiple trips to emergency to stop bleeding and even underwent emergency surgery for an acute subdural hematoma. It was a life-threatening condition, requiring immediate surgery. I still bear two small holes in my skull from where they drilled to drain the blood. Doctors eventually discovered that my heart was actually stopping for 15– 20 seconds before restarting. Two days later, now ten years ago, I received my first pacemaker!

The spirit to persevere is a God given gift and looking back, the only answer I have as to why I am still here is that God saved me for a reason. Just last week, I received my second pacemaker to keep my heart beating! So, today, I write and share with a grateful and beating heart — and yes, that, in itself, is another cause for my celebration!

What saddens me most these days is witnessing young lives cut short, or seeing the lack of understanding from younger people regarding the struggles elders have endured. At a time when love and compassion are most needed, it is disheartening to see burdens added to those who have already carried so much adversity.

I share these thoughts with humility and an open heart, holding that each day is still a gift from God. How we choose to use that gift is up to us. Forgiveness and grace are so important and are the gifts of those who truly understand their own worth. And, gratitude is the light that pierces even the darkest of circumstances. To live in gratitude is to live in that light.

We are all given the gift of choice, and that, too, is a cause for celebration! Life is far too short to take any moment for granted. I would be remiss if I didn't acknowledge the challenges of memory loss that come with age, something we all endure to varying degrees. So don't wait — embrace each new day as the precious gift it is, and let it be your reason for celebration! ❤️

Personal Reflections of Your Heart from This Essay

As you reflect on this essay, consider responding somehow to the following question: *What blessings in your life can you take a moment to celebrate today?*

30

LIVING A FULL AND VIRTUOUS LIFE

We are all explorers, endlessly discovering new heights
in the realms of life and understanding

Life is a constant journey of learning. Each of us has encountered countless experiences — successes, setbacks, and everything in between — each one adding to the mosaic of who we are today. Through these varied encounters, gaining the maturity that life's trials and triumphs bring, we grow in wisdom. In this way, we are all explorers, endlessly discovering new heights in the realms of life and understanding.

With a lifetime of experiences shaping my path, I find myself still marveling at the person I am and the role I can play. The notion of being "over the hill" has never quite sat right with me. Although my aspirations no longer revolve around high achievements or material success, my desires to be a good husband, have a positive influence, and make meaningful contributions to the world are as strong as ever.

Reflecting on my life now, I spend much of my time considering how to bring goodness into my relatively small circle. Not because I assume to know better, but because it's easy for any of us to lose sight of what truly matters amidst the hurry of modern life. Inspired by the timeless wisdom of those who have come before, I seek insights from thinkers and visionaries on what it means to live fully and virtuously. As Socrates said, *"The unexamined life is not worth living,"* reminding us that true growth begins with self-reflection.

A recurring theme in my reflections is the importance of self-awareness and personal improvement. By cultivating virtues like humility, compassion, and integrity, we create a foundation that enriches our lives and radiates outward. Marcus Aurelius noted, *"Waste no more time arguing about what a good man should be. Be one."* In striving to embody these values, we become better equipped to make a positive impact in our communities and the world.

Though I don't claim to have definitive answers, I am inspired by the wisdom of those who have left indelible marks on history, from Jesus to figures of our own era. They remind us to build lives anchored in love, empathy, and compassion, creating a world where justice, peace, and harmony are cherished. This enduring wisdom affirms that, by improving ourselves, we contribute to the betterment of society as a whole.

Helène and I, in our daily lives, strive to uphold these values, finding joy and gratitude in who we are and in the connections we cherish — with family, friends, and one another. The resilience and gratitude we cultivate help us navigate all challenges, holding fast to the belief that every day is a gift, rich with purpose. We create our reality through our choices, and with this perspective, why would we choose anything but happiness?

In embracing these virtues and insights, we not only live fuller lives but also become part of a legacy that transcends us, passing down a foundation of goodness for future generations. As Ralph Waldo Emerson put it, *"The purpose of life is not to be happy. It is to be useful, to be honorable, to be compassionate, to have it make some difference that you have lived and lived well."* May we each find our unique way to live well, leaving a trail of kindness, purpose, and hope for those who follow. ❤️

Personal Reflections of Your Heart from This Essay

As you reflect on this essay, consider responding somehow to the following question: *Are you someone who embraces the ups and downs of life in a way that spreads light in the world?*

31

THE QUALITY OF OUR PATH

Is shaped by faith, choices, and the love we share together and with others

Life is a tapestry woven from the threads of our choices and the beliefs that ground us. With every passing day, the decisions we make — or avoid — shape the landscape of our journey. More than external circumstances, it is our thoughts that fundamentally mold the quality of our experiences and our interactions with the world around us.

Given this profound truth, it becomes essential to guard and nurture our thoughts. What we think today becomes the reality we walk in tomorrow, and it has the potential to influence not only our own lives but also those we touch. Through my writing, I seek clarity and purpose, and in sharing these reflections, my hope is that my words might offer guidance or encouragement to someone searching for their own path, their sense of direction.

Regardless of one's religious beliefs or background, it is undeniable that religion can be a powerful source of guidance and renewal. Countless studies have shown a connection between religious engagement and positive health outcomes, including longevity. In our increasingly complex world, reconnecting with spiritual traditions can become a life-altering choice — one that offers solace and strength.

For instance, a 2016 study from Harvard T.H. Chan School of Public Health found that women who attended religious services more than once a week had a 33% lower risk of death compared to those who never attended. As noted in a 2018 *National Geographic* article, religious attendance has been linked to strengthened immune systems and extended lifespans. But beyond the science, the true value of religious participation lies in the rich sense of community, the deepening relationship with God, and embracing the Good News.

The Good News — the message of salvation through Jesus Christ — is central to Christian faith. It proclaims that God, in His infinite love, provided a path for humanity's reconciliation through the life, death, and resurrection of Christ. While early Christian teachings often used fear as a guiding force, the contemporary focus has shifted toward the transformative power of love, forgiveness, and grace. Modern Christianity emphasizes freedom, compassion, and inclusion — qualities that reflect the heart of Jesus' teachings.

In embracing this perspective, many churches today provide an enriching and expansive spiritual experience, fostering deeper connections with God and one another. Helène and I have found such a home at Trinity Lutheran Church on Whidbey Island, WA. It is a place where the positive message of the Gospel resonates not only within the walls of the sanctuary but also within the hearts of its members. Trinity is more than a Sunday gathering — it is a family of support, a beacon of shared values, and a source of strength as we navigate life's complexities.

As we journey through life, it becomes clear that our path is not just shaped by the events that unfold around us, but by how we choose to respond to them. Each thought, each decision, each act of love or kindness shapes our path — and the paths of others. *"Do not be conformed to this world, but be transformed by the renewal of your mind,"* writes Paul in Romans 12:2, reminding us that the quality of our life's journey begins with the transformation of our inner world.

Challenges, losses, and opportunities all come our way, but it is our response — rooted in free will — that determines the trajectory of our lives. What do you seek more of in your life? A community of love and support? The peace that comes with reconciliation with God? A deeper understanding of the Good News and its message of redemption and forgiveness? Or perhaps, simply, the possibility of living with greater joy and health?

Helène and I choose joy, love, and community every day. We find strength not only in our faith but also in the nurturing communities that surround us, extending far beyond Sunday mornings. We embrace each moment as a gift and an opportunity to walk a path illuminated by grace and gratitude.

As Proverbs 3:5-6 encourages us: *"Trust in the Lord with all your heart, and lean not on your own understanding; in all your ways submit to Him, and He will make your paths straight."* The quality of our path is ultimately shaped by our faith, our choices, and the love we share together and with others. ♥

Personal Reflections of Your Heart from This Essay

As you reflect on this essay, consider responding somehow to the following question: *What areas of your life have been transformed by your thoughts, and what areas might need transformation?*

32

THE WISDOM OF THE HEART

I consciously choose not to let age or infirmities
define who I am or hold me hostage

After almost 82 years, I still put myself out, contribute, make mistakes, and continue to learn and grow through it all. The words I share here give me a sense of purpose. My intention and hope are that something I've shared will make a positive difference for you. I'm grateful simply for the opportunity to share.

So I ask myself, am I speaking and writing from the wisdom of my heart or the learnedness or self-centeredness of my mind?

When I was much younger, I spoke more from my ego. I do not consider myself more intelligent or learned than anyone else. However, we represent a population of widely varied knowledge, intelligence, and accumulated wisdom. I am more willing than most to openly share my philosophical meanderings in the hope that something here will make a positive difference.

And yes, I get that you and most others reading this are already using your talents, experiences, and wisdom to make a positive difference in your life and in your own way. Writing is my way.

I have found these words from Michael Meade's writing in his Fate and Destiny to be meaningful: *"The passing of time makes everyone older, but not necessarily wiser."*

People either wise up to who they are at the core of their soul or else tend to slip into narrow, egocentric patterns. Either they develop a greater vision of life as they mature or they simply lose sight of who they were intended to be and what they came to give to the world.

Those old enough to know better would become living depositories of wisdom for the next generation to draw upon; if not, everyone would suffer a loss of knowledge and greater disorientation in the world. Having grown both older and wiser they knew best what needed to be preserved and remembered in order for human life to nobly and meaningfully proliferate in alignment with nature.

I cannot claim to live up to Meade's words, as I spent much of my earlier life consciously trying to fit in, to be "seen" as intelligent, and be accepted by others. Looking back, I see both the value and folly in doing so.

Perhaps some of that was necessary during my working years. And yet, at the time, speaking from my heart or drawing on my depository of wisdom was never a conscious consideration.

I have come to realize that it is not about what others think of me. What's most important is what I think of myself. Am I happy with myself, who I've become and who I'm being? I do not dwell on or allow past mistakes, or the opinion of others to shut me down or overshadow my goodness, loving nature or self-love!

No matter how we see the world, I believe each of us gains wisdom as we age. However, to me, it's more about owning it. Not flaunting it, and yet, not denying it.

Having lived through twelve years of severe, death-defying health issues, I believe I'm alive today for some greater purpose. *I consciously choose not to let age or infirmities define who I am or hold me hostage.* As such, I am determined to focus on continuing to serve others and make a difference during my remaining days. Hence my intention and hope that something here makes a positive difference for you.

Through all of this articulateness, what matters most to me is joy, laughter, love, and gratitude, with love the highest of all, especially for my amazing wife, Helène.

While you and I may not have met one another, each in our way, we are doing this life together! Hopefully, you have found something useful in these words and are already serving others from the wisdom of your heart! ♥️

Personal Reflections of Your Heart from This Essay

As you reflect on this essay, consider responding somehow to the following question: *What is one way you, with your unique talents and understanding, can give even more to the world than you already do?*

33

I SEE YOU: THE GIFT OF RECOGNITION AND PRESCENCE

A heartfelt 'I see you,' expressed through a kind word, a listening ear, or a shared moment of presence, is a profound gift to another

In a world where distractions pull us in countless directions, there is an extraordinary power in the simple act of truly "seeing" another person. To see someone, not just their face, but their essence, is to affirm their existence, their worth, and their place in the human family. This deep recognition, found in cultures across the world, is more than a greeting; it is an expression of presence, respect, and love.

The Zulu greeting *Sawubona*, meaning "I see you, " carries a profound significance. It does not merely acknowledge another's presence but recognizes their soul, their journey, and their intrinsic value. The traditional response, *Shikoba*, "I am here", completes the exchange, creating a sacred moment of connection. This concept echoes universal truths found in faith, philosophy, and the wisdom of human experience.

In the Bible, Jesus exemplifies this depth of vision. He saw those whom society overlooked — the poor, the sick, the brokenhearted — and in truly seeing them, He affirmed their worth. One of the most poignant examples is His encounter with Zacchaeus, the tax collector. While others dismissed Zacchaeus as a sinner, Jesus looked beyond the surface and called him by name, offering both recognition and redemption (Luke 19:1-10). To see with such clarity is to love as God loves, to look upon another with eyes of compassion and understanding.

The ability to see others deeply is an essential part of fostering meaningful relationships. In my years of working with men through the ManKind Project, I have witnessed the transformation that occurs when someone feels truly seen. When a person is met with open-hearted presence rather than judgment, they begin to step into their fullest self. It is a lesson that extends beyond personal encounters; it applies to how we engage with family, friends, and especially strangers.

As we age, the act of truly seeing becomes even more significant. Elders carry lifetimes of experiences, stories, and wisdom, yet in a society often focused on youth and productivity, they can sometimes feel invisible. A heartfelt "I see you" expressed through a kind word, a listening ear, or a shared moment of presence, is a profound gift to another. Likewise, younger generations, with their dreams and struggles, also need to be recognized and encouraged. By seeing each other across generations, we build bridges of understanding and honor the fullness of life's journey.

This practice of deep recognition is also essential in marriage and long-term partnerships. After decades together, it can be easy to assume we already know our beloved inside and out. Yet there is always more to see. Each day offers a new opportunity to witness our partner's kindness, strength, and growth. Helene and I have found that by truly seeing each other with fresh eyes, appreciating the small acts of love and the quiet moments of resilience, we continue to deepen our bond and celebrate the divine gift of our union.

Beyond human connection, to truly see another person is also to recognize the divine within them. There is a sacred mystery in the idea that within each person dwells the presence of God. This recognition calls us to a higher level of awareness, challenging us to treat each other with reverence, grace, and profound respect. When we see others in this light, our relationships are transformed, and our interactions become acts of sacred acknowledgment.

There is a story of a group of individuals struggling to find meaning, their relationships strained, their community fraying. An unexpected piece of wisdom comes to them: that among them is a person who carries within them the spirit of God in an extraordinary way. But they do not know who it is. This revelation changes the way they interact, for in every face, they begin to wonder, Is it this person? Their kindness deepens, their respect flourishes, and their community is renewed.

This wisdom applies to all of us. If we move through life with the awareness that each person we meet may hold a divine spark, our hearts open, our judgments soften, and our love expands. We see not just the human before us but the sacred within them. The beauty of this practice is that in doing so, we also allow others to see the sacred within us.

Seeing others is not limited to those we know personally; it extends to the world at large. When we recognize the humanity in every person we meet — the cashier at the store, the passerby on the street, the struggling soul who feels unseen — we participate in a quiet but profound act of healing. Every acknowledgment and every moment of presence contributes to a culture of kindness and belonging.

Maya Angelou said, *"I've learned that people will forget what you said, people will forget what you did, but people will never forget how you made them feel."* To truly see another person, to honor their existence and worth is one of the most powerful ways to communicate they are valued and loved.

May we go forth with open eyes and open hearts, practicing the sacred gift of recognition and seeing the divine within others. May we see and be seen. And in doing so, may we draw closer to the essence of God and love itself. *Sawubona!* ♥

Personal Reflections of Your Heart from This Essay

As you reflect on this essay, consider responding somehow to the following questions: What would it take for you to "see" somebody on a deeper level, who you normally would not "see" or talk to? What stops you from doing so?

NOTES OF APPRECIATION

Ron, you are a beacon of light in a (too often) dark world. – *Teri*

Ron – You help make each day more meaningful, significant and important. – *Matt*

Dear Ron, what valuable thoughts you have shared. Amazing clarity and no mincing of words. – *Karanth (Bangalore, India)*

Thank you, Ron. Your article benefits me, especially in terms of where I am currently in my life journey. – *June*

Ron, thank you for your positive thoughts. Your writing is a great reminder of the power of positive thoughts and gratefulness. – *Zim*

Ron, I LOVE your article!! Fantastic!! It is so packed with insights and thought provoking ideas! – *Julie B.*

Ron, what a magnificent gift you offer – a Divine way shower, one who assists others to make the journey a bit easier. You have just now assumed your position! It is one with great authority – almost like you have put on your royal robe and stepped up to the Throne – only it is a Divine Throne. You are very visible and will help people without knowing as they are observing you always. Your truth and caring make all want to listen to your wisdom. A great joyous journey awaits you. Know that you have earned your status and are Divinely supported. *Cynthia Cantor, Portland, OR 12/21/1995*

*Ron Roesler's
Sacred Geometry
Personal Power Symbol*

ABOUT THE AUTHOR

Ron Roesler's distinguished 30-year career at Chrysler Corporation exemplifies his resilience, leadership, and adaptability. Beginning as an hourly factory worker, Ron's journey through the ranks to the top 1% of the Company is a story of dedication and growth, ultimately reaching the Executive ranks at Chrysler's World Headquarters in Auburn Hills, Michigan.

A graduate of Central Michigan University with a Bachelor of Science in Corporate Leadership, Ron excelled as a Manager in Manufacturing, known for his forward-thinking strategies that fostered a culture of continuous improvement and teamwork.

Ron's tenure, starting in 1964 and spanning the transformative Iacocca recovery era of the late 1970s, was marked by a commitment to excellence. He led initiatives that not only strengthened team dynamics but also significantly enhanced quality and cost-effectiveness. His approach emphasized valuing each individual's potential, nurturing the strengths of subordinates, peers, and leaders alike.

After being promoted to the Corporate offices, as a creative contributor, Ron shared his insights in the Chrysler Times Company newsletters and lent his voice to Chrysler's leadership by ghostwriting speeches for Lee Iacocca. His innovative contributions and projects supporting the recovery efforts brought about substantial quality improvements and cost savings, earning him Chrysler's esteemed Chairman's Award, presented by Chairman Lee Iacocca himself, in recognition of his exceptional contributions.

Beyond his corporate achievements, Ron has consistently championed personal and community growth. As National Elder Chair for the ManKind Project (MKPUSA.org), he has supported MKP's mission to empower men to live responsibly and with integrity, fostering emotional maturity, spiritual depth, and community engagement.

As a lifelong Lutheran, his leadership extended to his faith community, where he served as President of his church's Leadership Council. During a critical pastoral transition, Ron stepped up as a lay minister, leading services, delivering sermons, and providing guidance to his congregation over an eighteen-month period.

In service to his community, Ron chaired Neighborhood Renaissance, Inc. (NRI), a non-profit organization dedicated to revitalizing a 39-block inner-city Detroit neighborhood. Collaborating with government, churches, and local services, NRI's efforts brought about tangible, positive change, culminating in the organization's recognition with a Presidential Point of Light award, presented by President George H.W. Bush in 1986.

"In every achievement I have been blessed to reach, I was fortunate to be surrounded by remarkable and energized people. Their dedication, vision, and contributions made each accomplishment not only possible but meaningful. I stand here today not solely through my own efforts, but because of the combined strength, support, and commitment of those who shared in the journey. I am deeply grateful for their presence. Without them, none of these accomplishments would have happened.

Now at 84, I channel my lifetime of insights into writings on aging, resilience, and the power of a positive outlook. I embrace both successes and setbacks as opportunities for growth, continually advocating for perseverance, lifelong learning, forgiveness, and a commitment to contributing to a better world." ♥

www.ingramcontent.com/pod-product-compliance
Lightning Source LLC
Chambersburg PA
CBHW051213120626
46547CB00013B/1335